Dedication

This book is dedicated to my niece Patricia "Trish" Taft of Newport, Rhode Island and Baker's Island, Massachusetts. Trish doesn't believe in ghosts, probably because she has such a lively spirit of her own, but she did a fine job for me in tracking down haunted houses to explore.

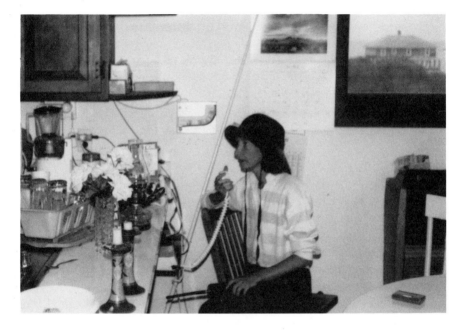

Trish Cahill Taft at her radio post as caretaker of Baker's Island off the coast of Manchester-by-the-Sea. She lives on the island in the winter and is responsible for security and maintenance of the lighthouse and sixty summer cottages—a few of which are haunted.

©Copyright, Old Saltbox, 1992 ISBN - 0-9626162-3-0

COVER PHOTO: An oil painting by Trish Cahill Taft of the haunted porch overlooking the sea and Halfway Rock at Baker's Island. Photo by Steve Harwood, courtesy of Richard and Susan Dionne. Trish titled her painting: "Halfway Rocker".

INTRODUCTION

Are there ghosts or aren't there ghosts? Wouldn't you really like to know? I saw a ghost once, or I think I did, and it frightened me so much as it approached my bedside that when I screamed, no sound came out of my mouth. I was 20 years old then and I'm much older now, but ghosts still make me feel uncomfortable. Yet, today I go out looking for them.

Mysteries have always intrigued me, to the point where I am determined to solve them, or at least attempt to do so. Like Don Quixote I set out on a quest in New England to see if I could unravel the mystery of hauntings. Accompanying me on most of these sojourns was Brian-the-monk, a lay-Franciscan who did a remarkable job of capturing some of these elusive spirits on film. Our odyssey wasn't as much frightening as it was fascinating. We did, however, have a few creepy experiences, as well as a few laughs, and we met a lot of interesting people.

If the physiological sensations that both Brian and I experienced in these haunted places were not inspired by spirits, then there has to be some other explanation for them, but I can't begin to understand what it might be. The electric pins and needles sensations I got while visiting these places was not the result of nervousness or fear, but was an instinctive sensitivity unleashed from within me when in the presence of unseen spirits. Brian's resultant photographs added credence to these instincts, seemingly justifying my conclusion that we were indeed among spirits.

I have little trouble believing that my spirit will live on after I die. Even Einstein convinced other scientists that energy cannot die, and you and I are energy. I also believe in the Holy-Spirit of the God-Christ trilogy, and that my spirit will lodge itself in the appropriate bin either heaven or hell when the time comes. I do, however, find it difficult to believe that after-death spirits remain floating about this world, not able, or possibly not willing, to find their niche in the worlds beyond. But then, if these are not restless spirits, what are they? Some believe that ghosts are merely figments of the imagination, illusions based on unfounded superstitions, hallucinations, or dreams and nightmares that only seem real. Possibly, what are thought to be hauntings, are merely the residue of intense emotions, feelings, or something experienced by someone on a particular spot or in a specific place many years before. My dilemma is that I find it just as difficult to believe in ghosts as I find it difficult to disbelieve in them. The question of ghosts has, of course, perplexed living souls since shortly after Adam and Eve, and we seem no closer to an answer now than they did then.

Brian-the-monk believes that all ghosts are evil, or at least, should be approached with suspicion. I have a strong respect and fear of things demonic and feel that they should be avoided at all costs. I think ghosts for the most part must be merely lost souls, trapped in a kind of time warp, probably not knowing how to proceed into the next world. Maybe they don't want to make a move, realizing that from past living exploits their only egress is to head down. Or they might feel that they have some important unfinished business here. But, whichever, this little book should entertain you and, hopefully, give you further insight into the realm of the unknown. It will also provide you with a unique history concerning our forever haunting and mysterious New England.

Bob Cahill

Brian, the man who took the infra-red photos of ghosts for this book, is a Franciscan lay-monk and, therefore, wishes to remain anonymous. Here he snaps a photo of himself in an antique mirror hanging on the wall of the haunted dining room at John Stone's Inn, Ashland, MA.

Al Janard, Larry Gallagher and Mike Chandler metal detecting at Portland, Maine before catching the ferry to Nova Scotia, where ghost fever rather than treasure fever plagued them.

I
Fire Fiend of Amherst

My intention to visit Nova Scotia in April was to search for lost ancestors that may have arrived in Canada in the mid-1800s aboard *"Coffin ships"* from Ireland. Legend within the Cahill family was that close relatives of my great-grandfather Michael, of Kilworth, County Cork, made it safely to the shores of Nova Scotia during the potato famine and remained in Canada for the rest of their lives. I had visited Kilworth in Ireland a few years earlier and found further evidence of a mass migration from that village in the mid-1800s to the Maritime Provinces of Canada. I was told that the Canadians keep impeccable records of immigration, and so I was anxious to research their files.

My friend Al Janard decided to join me on my week-long visit north because he had always wanted to go metal detecting in Canada, which he considered virgin territory for an experienced coin-shooter. Al was also excited about the possibility of stopping at Oak Island, just south of Halifax, where, supposedly, a great treasure was buried in the early 1700s and hunters have been attempting to dig it out for well over 250 years. My childhood pal, Larry Gallagher, a local restauranteur also wanted to come along, not only to get a respite from a grueling winter spent bending over a hot stove, but to taste the reputed good food of the elegant restaurants of Halifax. To complete our quartet of foreign travelers, a young man named Mike Chandler, some 15 years our junior, joined us, for no other reason than to get away after a long, snowy New England winter. On the overnight car-ferry from Portland, Maine, to Yarmouth, Nova Scotia, Gallagher and Chandler got seasick just as we all sat down for dinner, which, of course, ruined everyone's meal. This seemed to set the pattern for our Canadian vacation—just the first of many curses.

After landing in the early morning at Yarmouth, we spent the next two days driving from village to village up the western shore. These days were completely uneventful. The people were polite and kind but of little help. There was no information on Irish, let alone Cahills, coming into this area of Nova Scotia; metal detecting was poor, not even a buzz on Al's machine to stimulate his heartbeat; and there wasn't one restaurant that delighted Gallagher's palate. When we arrived in Halifax, we were told that we should have traveled up the east coast and not the west to have found the best scenery, restaurants, research libraries and pirate treasure coves. Our intent was to return by that route.

We visited Oak Island to please Al Janard, but we weren't allowed to step foot on the island, because professional treasure hunters were bulldozing the area in pursuit of the elusive treasure, and we would just be in the way. Al was disappointed. We did, however, eat good meals in Halifax, the capitol of Nova Scotia, which seemed to somewhat calm Gallagher's increasingly hostile temperament. He announced at our final dinner in Halifax that he did not want to return to Maine and America via the ferry, for obvious reasons, but he decided that we should take the long route home, driving through New Brunswick. Chandler, who had also been seasick on the ferry, did not object, and Al, who thought Saint John, the capitol of New Brunswick, might be a good place to hunt for coins with his metal detector, also agreed to the new plan. I, on the other hand, was a bit reluctant, for I had found no information on Cahills in the Halifax archives and thought the village libraries and historical societies on the east coast of Nova Scotia might provide me with information on the Kilworth immigrants. Gallagher was emphatic. If we went down the east coast, we would be obliged to take the ferry at Yarmouth to return home, and he would never take that ferry again. Gallagher and I were at an impasse, and Al called for a compromise. He knew I had an interest in ghosts, and he had once heard the most horrifying ghost story ever about a haunted house in Amherst, Nova Scotia, located on the New Brunswick border.

"Since we're going that way, we can stop there and visit it," Al suggested.

"If we go that way, we won't have time for a stopover," said Gallagher. *"I've got to get back to my restaurant, and going this way will take us a lot longer to get home."*

Gallagher had never appreciated my interest in the supernatural. He didn't want to get bogged down in still another boring village while I chased down a story. Al and Mike, however, thought a little ghost-busting might add some excitement to what had thusfar been an uneventful trip. If we weren't going the Yarmouth route then we had to stop at Amherst, or I wouldn't agree with the change in plans, and I had to be given two hours in the library to research this ghost before we left Halifax. Al assured me that it was a notorious haunting about the turn of the century and that the Halifax Library should have information on it.

"Only one hour at the library and only one hour in Amherst," Gallagher reluctantly relented.

Gallagher said his concern for time was *"night driving, and daylight was needed to find a good hotel in Saint John, New Brunswick, before darkness set in the following night."* I was up early and at the library before Gallagher woke up, and back at the hotel and ready to go before they all had finished breakfast. Old newspaper articles had given me the information I wanted.

I waited until we were on the road, with Gallagher at the wheel, to reveal the nightmarish truth I had uncovered at the library. Since the time we were kids growing up in Salem, Massachusetts, Larry Gallagher had tried to conceal from me and others his terrible fear of ghosts. I had relished telling spooky tales to my jittery friend, who had always blocked his ears or left the room on some pretense before I finished my stories. Now, as he hugged the wheel during our drive

5

through the Nova Scotia wilderness, I told him what I had learned that morning at the library about the fiendish spirit that haunted the cottage at 16 Princess Street, Amherst. I knew that, even though Gallagher was now in his early fifties, I could still scare the pants off him.

"*Esther Cox, a short stout girl, just out of her teens,*" I began, "*lived with her married sister and brother-in-law, Daniel Teed, over his shoemaker shop, right in the downtown area of the village of Amherst. Esther, on the evening of September Fourth, 1878, had gone on a buggyride with a boy named Bob, also a shoemaker. According to newspaper reports, Bob had become overly aggressive with her that evening, even brutal. They quarreled and Bob brought her back home to Princess Street. She entered the house in a near state of panic. A few moments later Bob was killed in a gruesome accident. He had fallen forward off his buggy, and was crushed under the hoofs and wheels of his own coach and team. Esther didn't hear of Bob's tragic death 'til the next morning, but that evening, as she and her older sister Jennie went to sleep, they heard thumping noises under their bed. They screamed for their brother-in-law, Dan Teed, to come into the room to rid it of what they thought was a mouse.*" As I told the story, I stared at Gallagher. He had his eyes on the road, seemingly absorbed in his own thoughts, but his long face had begun to pale and his fingers noticeably tightened on the steering wheel. There was no way to block his ears this time, nor could he escape the confines of the car.

"*Dan Teed could find no mouse in their room. Esther, however, was now trembling with a fever. A few hours later, her legs began to swell and she was screaming with pain. The village doctor Thomas Carrittee was called. When he entered Esther's bedroom, the bedclothes flew off her body and her pillow was thrown at the doctor, as if by some unseen hand. Esther just laid helpless, groaning in bed. Then Esther's bed began to shake. In the room with Esther, at the time, were Dan Teed, her sister, her brother Bill Cox, who also lived in the house, and the doctor. All of them saw words being slowly and deeply scratched into the plaster wall above Esther's head by an invisible hand wielding an invisible cutting tool. The final etched message read: 'Esther Cox, you are mine to kill!' With the shock of this fresh in their minds, a voice cried out from within the room, which Esther later said sounded like her boyfriend Bob's voice: 'Your house will be set afire.' The hollow voice seemed to come from nowhere. Lighted matches then fell from the ceiling to the floor, littering the bedroom. They all ran around stomping and snuffing them out. Then Dan Teed ran downstairs, for he smelled smoke coming from the cellar. There, he found woodchips aflame. He quickly extinguished them, only to be driven out of the cellar by flying shovels and hoes. The Teeds gathered in the living room, debating whether or not they should leave their home. There were no other strange occurences that day, nor for four days thereafter, although the family got little sleep those nights, anticipating another encounter with the ghost.*"

"It's not a ghost," Al corrected me, "it's a poltergeist."

"I don't want to hear anymore about it!" said Gallagher.

"Four nights later, Esther got sick again, but the swelling of her legs was not as bad. A kerosene lamp was going, and four other members of the family were in her bedroom when her bedclothes flew off her. Mrs. Teed covered her but the bedclothes instantly flew off her again. Jennie Cox fainted when loud banging like thunder came from under the bed, and the room began to shake. Dan Teed thought his house had been hit by lightning, but there was no storm outside. Great clashes of thunder were coming from under the bed. Doctor Carrittee was called in again, and he described the sounds as 'like fireworks.' The explosions continued for over two hours, and the doctor then concluded that Esther was haunted by demons. As exhausted as she was, she of course, got little sleep during all of this. She complained of the feeling of electricity passing through her body, and a painful movement in her stomach. The doctor gave her morphine to calm her nerves, and when she finally slept, the sound of pounding moved from under her bed to the roof of the house. 'It sounded like there was a man up there with a heavy sledgehammer,' the local newspaper reported, and now, of course, the entire village was aroused. The next day, the pounding started in the early morning and lasted all day. Many people came to look, but no one saw anyone on the roof."

"You say anymore and I won't turn off the road to Amherst," said Gallagher. I smiled at him. "I mean it!" he said. I kept quiet.

He grudgingly pulled off the highway before we entered New Brunswick and drove down a narrow winding road, following an old road sign that read "Amherst." We saw three young boys with books under their arms. Gallagher stopped beside them.

"How far to downtown Amherst?" he asked.

"Less than a mile," replied one of the schoolboys.

"Ever hear of the Amherst ghost?" I asked them before Gallagher could pull away.

"You mean the Amherst Mystery," they corrected me.

"The old house is gone," one of them informed us. "It was torn down some years back."

"No one would live in it," smiled the smallest of the lot.

"It used to stand on the corner of Main and Princess Streets," one explained, "across from the Lady Amherst Restaurant."

The word restaurant gave Gallagher new energy. We thanked the boys and drove on.

The village center was but two main thoroughfares, with Princess Street connecting them. On the corner of Main was a grassy plot, flanked by a one-story brick building and a cement block building, both housing local businesses. The location of the old haunted house was highly conspicuous with a waist high picket fence closing in the empty lot—obviously nobody dared rebuild there.

"Nothing here," Gallagher smiled at the rest of us, *"let's go eat."*

I decided I wanted a photo of my traveling companions standing in front of the grassy plot where the haunted cottage once stood and under the road sign that read *"Princess Street."* Al and Mike were willing to pose, but Gallagher, his coat collar pulled up around his ears to block out the chill wind, headed across the street to the *"Lady Amherst."* I had only two photos left on the roll. I stood on the opposite curb and aimed the camera at Mike and Al hugging the street sign pole. Be it a gust of wind, a slip of the foot, or the push from some unseen hand, I know not, but as I snapped the photo, I went sprawling head first onto the cobblestone street. The camera flew from my hands and bounced across the street, pieces flying off on impact, and the automatic flash started clicking on and off non-stop. Except for a scraped elbow and a very sore knee, I survived the fall, but the camera didn't. Al came running over to me.

"What happened?" he asked? *"It looked like you got kicked in the rear end by an invisible foot."*

And maybe that's just what did happen. Gallagher, now standing in the middle of Main Street with his hands on his hips, shouted. *"I suppose you're going to blame that on the ghost!"*

As we headed into the village restaurant, I quickly rolled up the film, took it out of the camera, stuffed it into my coat pocket and zipped up the pocket as added protection for the film. I, hopefully, had gotten a photo and had not exposed the film during the accident, but I wouldn't know that for sure 'til I got the film developed.

The dining room of the *"Lady Amherst"* was surprisingly large for a village restaurant, but it was dark and there wasn't another person in the room. As we sat at a huge round table, a waitress appeared out of the gloom. As she took our order I asked her if she knew anything about the house that once stood across the street. She smiled.

"It was torn down because it was haunted." she said, *"and there are many here in town who think the corner lot where the house stood is still haunted."*

"They're right," said Al Janard. Gallagher scoffed.

"I don't know much more about it," the waitress continued, *"but there is a reproduction of an old testimony concerning it tacked to the wall over there."*

She pointed across the room. I immediately got up and walked across the room to read the two frayed copies of what was once a newspaper article. It was dated June 1908, and read as follows:

8

"We the undersigned inhabitants of the Town of Amherst, County of Cumberland, Nova Scotia and Dominion of Canada, having our own personal knowledge and not be or through hearsay of belief absolutely known, seen and heard individually all or some of the demonstrations, manifestation and communication of an invisible, intelligent and malicious power within the atmosphere, that continued its awe inspiring mysterious operations in the home of Daniel Teed, 16 Princess Street, Amherst, and elsewhere in the actual presence of his sister-in-law, Esther Cox, but never manifested itself during her absence from the house, but continued to manifest itself for the period of one year 1878 - 1879..."

The yellowed reproduction of the document, obviously a newspaper copy, was signed by 16 residents of Amherst, the first being Daniel Teed. Beside it hung another copy of a document, signed only by Daniel Teed. It read: *"In the house where my terrible experience occurred, horrors in the forms too monstrous for belief lurked within the atmosphere, the kindling of mysterious fires struck terrors in the hearts of all; the trembling and shaking of the house and the creaking of the walls, the fearful pounding; and other weird noises, as if made by invisible sledgehammers upon the roof, walls and floor; the strange actions of the household furniture which moved about in broad daylight; the shrill and awful voices in the air; and the terrifying legend written on the wall... and I claim that the power producing these weird results was in the instance that came under my personal observation, nothing more or less than ghosts of the dead."*

Gallagher finished his sandwich before the rest of us and was anxious to begin our 140 mile trek to Saint John. As we were about to leave, the waitress told me that the local bookstore located around the corner sold a little pamphlet on the subject. I rushed down the street to the bookstore as the others headed back to the car, Gallagher glancing at his watch impatiently. I was back in a flash, having purchased a copy of *"The Great Amherst Mystery,"* by Walter Hubbell, printed in 1888. As we headed out to the highway, with Gallagher speeding to hopefully reach Saint John before nightfall, I read excerpts aloud from the pamphlet. Walter Hubbell, a skeptic much like Gallagher, had been traveling through Canada as a Shakespearian actor when he visited Dan Teed And Esther Cox in 1878.

"I was just inside the house and had only been seated for a moment," writes Hubbell, *"when my satchel was thrown across the room, and at the same instant, a large chair came rushing from the opposite side of the room, striking the one on which I was seated with such a tremendous force that it was nearly knocked from under me. It was early morning....I was a skeptic no longer, but was convinced that there is an invisible power within the atmosphere that men have so far failed to comprehend, and that at last it had struck me like a*

cyclone.... The table knives were then thrown on the floor, the chairs pitched over, and after breakfast the dining table fell over on its side, rugs upon the floor were slid about, and the whole room literally turned into a pandemonium, so filled with dust that I went into the parlor...

While on the sofa in the parlor in the afternoon, several knitting needles were taken from the knitting in Esther's hands and thrown at me. A piece of cake little George (Mrs. Teed's five year old son) was eating, was snatched by the ghost from his hand and thrown at me three times in succession. Dear little fellow, he cried bitterly about it. The ghost then undressed George by tearing his clothes off, after unbuttoning them, at which rough treatment he cried again. I believe he could at times see the ghost, for more than once I observed that he acted as if a stranger was present whom he feared. On that same day, Esther's face was slapped by the ghost, so that the mark of fingers could be plainly seen just exactly as if a human hand had slapped her face; these slaps could be plainly heard by all present. I heard them distinctly, time and again....Late in the afternoon the ghost set some old newspapers on fire upstairs, the burning papers were extinguished, however, without any serious damage being done to the house or furniture. This was my first experience with Bob the demon as a fire fiend....The first inclination we would have was the smell of smoke pouring through the house, and then everybody began running with buckets of water, the most awful calamity that could befall any family."

"*Oh no!*" shouted Al Janard from the back seat of the car, interrupting my reading, "*My watch has stopped.*" He pressed his wrist to his ear.

"*So what?*" said Gallagher.

"*I've had this Timex since I was a young man. I've worn it most of my life, and it's never failed me....And look at the time it stopped,*" he shouted, passing the watch around the car to show us all. "*It's four-twenty, exactly the time you were taking our picture and fell on your face in the street.*" Al and Mike stared at me wide-eyed from the back seat.

"*You guys are all nuts,*" said Gallagher. "*So your watch stopped exactly the time Cahill took your photo. So, a gust of wind knocks Cahill into the street—it's all coincidental.*"

"*I just hope that the photo I took on Princess Street comes out,*" I said to Gallagher, "*and I hope the ghost is there standing next to Al and Mike for you to see, Larry.*"

I patted my coat pocket, and then near-panic set in, for there was no familiar bump in the pocket. I quickly unzipped it—the pocket was empty. I checked my other pockets, my overnight bag, the car seat—my roll of film was gone. This seemed impossible to me. I had deposited all my completed film rolls into this same coat pocket during our trip, then placed them in my overnight bag at the end of each day. Then I noticed that there was a razor-thin tear in the bottom of

10

my coat pocket. It hadn't been there earlier, and possibly was caused when I fell onto Princess Street, meaning that my roll of film was on the street in Amherst. We were already two hours closer to Saint John, New Brunswick. We all agreed it was too late to turn around and try to retrieve the roll of film. The sun was setting as we entered Saint John. I thought it a dismal looking city. We all sat silently contemplating our unusual day. Gallagher considered the accident on Princess Street, the failed watch and the lost film, all coincidental, and maybe he was right. But Al, Mike and I had our doubts.

Al had spotted a park near a waterfall close to the hotel we stayed at that night, and he wanted to search it with his metal detector next morning. Mike wanted to shop, and I wanted to spend some time at the Saint John Library checking on Irish immigration in my pursuit of Cahills. Larry was, therefore, outvoted in his suggestion that we leave early for our drive to the American border and home. We all agreed that we would leave at noon. The librarian referred me to the New Brunswick Museum on Douglas Street, where I found the archivist and her assistants most helpful. Saint John had been the major destination for most Irish coming into Canada in the nineteenth century. This museum's files were the most organized and detailed that I had ever found in all my years of genealogical research: Of the total immigration into New Brunswick from 1812 to 1850, 71% had been from Ireland, and from 1844 to 1847, 33,000 Irish arrived at Saint John to a city population of 30,000. Many, sadly, died in a smallpox epidemic, some were shipwrecked, but the museum had compiled a list of all the living and the dead. To my astonishment, there wasn't a Cahill among them. I was late meeting the others back at the hotel. Gallagher was impatient. I was angry and disappointed at not finding a trace of my ancestors. I informed Gallagher that although I hadn't found one Cahill, I had counted thirty-six Gallaghers that had entered Saint John in the last century. He wasn't interested.

To fill the eight monotonous hours of driving from New Brunswick and down the entire coast of Maine to Salem, Massachusetts I read aloud from Walter Hubbell's personal experiences at the house on Princess Street:

"About one month after the commencement of the wonders," wrote Hubbell, *"Reverend Edwin Clay, a well know Baptist clergyman, called at the house to see and hear the wonders of which he had read some accounts in the newspapers but was desirous of seeing and hearing for himself; and he was fortunate enough to have his desires gratified by hearing the loudest kinds of sounds, and seeing the writing on the wall. When he left the house he was fully satisfied that Esther did not in any way produce the sounds herself, and that the family had nothing whatever to do with them."*

He, however, agreed with Dr. Carrittee in his theory that her nerves had received a shock of some kind, making her in some mysterious manner an electric battery. His idea being that invisible flashes of lightning left her person and that the sounds which every person could hear so distinctly, were minute peals of thunder... *"When the inhabitants of Amherst heard that such eminent and worthy men as Rev. Dr. Edwin Clay and the genial and ever popular Dr. Carrittee, took an interest in the haunted house of Daniel Teed, it became fashionable for even the most exclusive class to call at the cottage to hear and see the wonders...Often while the house was filled with visitors, large crowds would stand outside unable to gain admittance because there was not enough room inside. On several occasions the Amherst police force had to be called to keep order....*

All the family were not fully convinced the mysterious power was really what it claimed to be, the ghost of some very evil man, who, in some unknown manner managed to torture poor Esther, as only such a ghost would....Daniel Teed, explained to me the true nature of the torture, but it must be nameless here...The ghost had actually talked to Esther and told her that his name was Bob and that there was a second ghost in the house called Maggie. Together, he whispered to Esther, they planned on burning down the house while all were asleep."

Doctor Carrittee continued to visit the Teed home every day, mainly to give Esther sedatives. She eventually contracted diphtheria and was bedridden for many weeks, but during that time, strangely enough, the ghosts of Bob and Maggie didn't torment her. Hubbell concluded that the power of the poltergeists seemed to increase during a 28 day period, then subside and slowly increase every 28 days, like the phases of the moon—their mischief reaching a zenith during the full moon. Little fires were continuously being set throughout the house, and *"Daniel Teed and his wife were afraid that the ghost would start a fire in some inaccessible place, where it could not be extinguished"* wrote Hubbell. One fire that started in a barrel of shavings in the cellar, *"aroused the entire neighborhood,"* and although it was extinguished, the local newspaper wrote about the incident, mentioning that the fire was thought to be started by ghosts. Many skeptics who had already concluded that Esther Cox was demented or having delusions, now considered her to be a dangerous firebug. As Hubbell explains:

"If Daniel Teed's cottage caught fire while the wind was blowing from the bay when it would be most favorable for such a terrible catastrophe, nothing could possibly save the little village from being reduced to ashes. As if to pile horror upon horror, one night while Esther and the entire family were sitting in the parlor the ghost became visible to her. When she saw him first she started to her feet and seemed about to fall dead from fright. Recovering her strength and selfpossession in a moment, however, she pointed to a distant corner of the room with her trembling hand, and exclaimed in a hoarse and broken voice: 'Look there! My God it is the ghost, Don't you all see him too? There he stands, his

eyes are glaring, and he laughs at me and says I must leave this house tonight, or he will kindle a fire in the loft under the roof and burn us all to death. Oh! what shall I do? Where shall I go? The ground is covered with snow, and yet I must not remain here, for he will do what he threatens, he always does.' Then she fell to the floor, in agony of grief and fear, weeping aloud for a moment, and then all was still..."

Dan Teed discovered to his dismay that no village neighbor would take Esther in. But a farmer, John White, who had an interest in the supernatural and lived some three miles from the village, was willing to board Esther for two weeks. He also owned a *"dining saloon"* in the village, possibly where the *"Lady Amherst"* stands today, and he agreed to have Esther work there. For twelve days Esther had no problems or visitations at the White's farm-house, but on the following day, while scrubbing the floor, the ghost took the scrubbing brush from her hand. She screamed and the Whites arrived on the scene, all to witness the scrub brush fall from the ceiling. Then the heavy iron door of the cooking stove started slamming until it was knocked off its hinges and went flying across the kitchen floor. It took two men to replace the door to the stove, but the moment it was reattached, it came off and went flying across the room again. Then a knife was lifted from the counter and it stabbed Esther. The loud knocking began on the roof like at Teed's house, and Esther was sent to another family in Saint John. The ghost, Bob, went with her.

Esther stayed with a family named VanAmburgh, living some three miles outside the city. She remained there for eight weeks, until the VanAmburghs could stand the loud banging on the roof of their home no longer. The ghost had also attacked their cat and tried to kill it, so Esther returned to Amherst and Dan Teed's house, where all had been tranquil during her absence. At the Teeds, it seems that Maggie the ghost joined Bob again. *"Bob and Maggie were both continually stealing small articles,"* wrote Hubbell, *"and after keeping them for days and sometimes weeks, would suddenly let them fall out of the air upon the floor. This we saw time after time....Sofas and tables were continually turned upside down, knives and forks thrown with such force that they would stick into doors, food disappeared from the table, and worse than all, strange unnatural voices could be heard in the air, calling us by our names. William Cox and John Teed left the house for good—driven away."*

One Sunday Esther went to the Amherst Episcopal church with others in the Teed household, but as Hubbell relates, *"the demon followed her and created so much disturbance that we were compelled to leave."* Every time the minister, Reverend Temple, mentioned Satan or the Holy Ghost, *"this demon Bob, would knock on the floor or the back of the pew. He finally upset the kneeling stool and commenced to throw the hymn book about. The congregation was greatly*

13

disturbed and Esther became crimson with mortification."

Mrs. Teed relates, *"On Sunday night after we were all in bed, Esther being in her own room, opposite mine and Mr. Teed's, our doors were both open and we could both look into her room for it was moonlight. We saw a chair slide across her room from the wall and when it was near her and close up to it, the pillow under her head came out and settled down on the chair. Esther could see Maggie the ghost, dressed all in white, sit down on the pillow on the chair, but we could not see her at all. Maggie then rubbed Esther from head to foot under the bedclothes and then began to pinch her on the arms and neck, and then scratch her body with a hairpin we found in the bed next day. Esther said she could not stand it any longer. Bob the ghost, then got to work and threw all the furniture except the bedstead out of the room into the entry. Esther could see him do it. We could only see the things come out and see that she lay in bed still and quiet. After the furniture had been all thrown out of the room, Bob commenced to rock and shake the bed as Esther lay there in it. The noise was so great we could not sleep, so Mr. Teed, at my request went into her room and took Esther's mattress off her bed and brought it into our room where he put it on the floor at the foot of our bed so we could all go to sleep....All the demons could work better in our cottage on Princess Street than anywhere else, and they were afraid to do much in a room where Mr. Teed was, because they did not want him to say Esther must go away for fear all would be burned up by Bob as we nearly were. After the mattress had been brought into our room and Esther was lying on it, the ghosts took hold of the lid of an old trunk in our room that was not locked but shut down and gave it just one parting slam as a good night, nothing else occurred and we all went to sleep in peace."*

Walter Hubbell, after spending many weeks at the Teed cottage, left to continue on with his acting career, and the Teeds, unwilling to cope with the antics of the ghosts any longer, shipped Esther back to the VanAmburgh's While there, a neighbor's barn caught on fire and burned to the ground. Since Esther had visited the barn earlier on the day of the fire, she was accused of setting it, was taken to court, found guilty, and sentenced to four months in jail. She was released from jail after a month and returned to Amherst, where she married two years later and bore a son, but her husband died shortly thereafter.

The publication **Banner of Light** of Boston, in its July 12, 1883 issue, states that, *"Esther has not been tormented since her marriage."* After her husband's death, she lived for a while with her baby at East Machias, Maine at the home of her father, Archibald Cox. She remarried a few years later and moved to Brockton Massachusetts, where she, apparently, lived happily and unmolested into old age.

We arrived in Salem, Massachusetts, after our long tiresome ride from Saint

14

John, New Brunswick. I was the first to be dropped off, and Larry, Mike and Al came into the house for a cup of coffee. My wife Sandy was anxious to hear about our trip, but all, including myself, had little to say.

"You all look like you've seen a ghost," said Sandy and at that, the boys gulped down their coffee and left for their respective homes. Sandy was mystified. *"Did I say something wrong?"* she asked me.

"No," I replied. *"It was just a long tiring trip, and we did have a little brush with what might be construed as a ghost."*

She wanted to know more, and after talking about the Amherst ghosts all the way from Saint John, I wasn't in the mood to explain it all to her. She insisted on knowing more, so I took out Hubbell's pamphlet.

"Maybe he has a summary at the end of the booklet," I told her, and *"If so, I'll read it to you, but otherwise, it's too long and complicated a story to talk about now."*

The last page of Hubbell's pamphlet did have, what I thought was, a synopsis. It's title was: *'Thirty Years After—1908.'* I began reading aloud:

"After closing the season in Yarmouth, my supporting company returned to the United States and I went to .... Amherst .... I have now been living in Amherst for three weeks and during that time have slept in the same room of dreadful recollections. If the walls or rooms could only talk or show again in awful scenes and deeds enacted in them, the sufferings of Esther Cox, in this my present bedroom would probably give me the nightmare of some other kinds of phantasmagoria or hallucination every night, but I am sure they cannot speak in any way or form but are as silent as the eternal silence of a tomb, because I sleep well. It has interested me to ascertain the past history of the cottage.....After Daniel Teed moved away and then died here himself about fifteen years ago, he left Robert W. Davis his stepson who lived with him in the house in possession. The next tenant was Mrs. Rebecca Cahill who has lived here about ten years...."

I stopped, and read the last sentence again. Chills flooded my body. Sandy stared wide-eyed as the hairs on my arms stood on end. Here were the Cahills— the ones I had searched for in vain throughout Nova Scotia and New Brunswick—they lived in the house after the Teeds! I quickly read on:

"Mrs. Cahill's household consists of her son Mr. John Cahill, his wife Mrs. Myrtle Cahill, and dear little daughter Audrey, one year old, and grown up daughter, Miss Sadie May Betts, and it is due entirely to their kindness that I am allowed to rent this room. I came to them a stranger and they took me in. Mr. Cahill's room is the one at the head of the stairway. It is the one in which the ghosts first demonstrated their awe-inspiring power and it was upon the walls of that room that Bob the demon ghost, fire-fiend and tormentor of the household wrote with the iron spike that terrifying legend, 'Esther Cox you are mine to kill...' he wrote upon the bare plaster of the wall. Hundreds of persons read it as

15

I did many times. On examining the walls on which it had been written, to my great disappointment it had been covered over with paper. At my suggestion Mr. Cahill had the wall paper removed from the wall which we then examined and found that the room had been re-papered four or five times and that the wall itself had been given a heavy coating of white paint, apparently to cover, hide and obliterate the legend...."

Hubbell then writes that he believed the demon ghosts were finally frightened away from the house, or at least from Esther, by a Micmac Indian Witch Doctor, who came to Amherst to cure Esther. Whatever the reason, the ghosts ceased their mischief about one year after they had first appeared. Why the Cahills moved into a house which they knew was haunted, I find hard to understand, and why was the house torn down if it was still considered liveable after all that demonic activity? It was obvious to me while visiting Amherst that no one dared build on the grassy lot surrounded by a white picket fence in the downtown area. The question of the Cahill family still haunts me to this day.

As Al Janard concluded: *"The wind could have blown you down on the street while you were taking the photo, my watch could have stopped at that moment on its own, and you could have lost the film by chance or by mistake. But after all the time and effort you spent trying to find lost members of the Cahill clan and finding out once you got home that they actually lived in that haunted house, that seems beyond being coincidence."*

I agreed!

This portrait of Eunice Turner Balston, granddaughter of John Turner, the man who built the House Of Seven Gables in 1668, now hangs in the parlor of the house. Her father and brother, John Turner II and III, once owned Baker's Island at the mouth of Salem Bay, but her family was forced to sell the island in 1770 for needed cash. While visiting this house made famous by Salem novelist Nathaniel Hawthorne, professional photographer Duane Eichholtz took this photo of the portrait, not realizing that he was also capturing a demonic looking ghost standing behind Mrs. Balston.

A hooded figure, supposedly the ghost of a monk, stands in the original Witch Dungeon and Jail in Salem. The photo was taken sometime near the turn of the last century.

Photo courtesy of Henry Theriault-Seawitch.

Here at the Howard Street Burying Ground, with the abandoned Salem Jail and Sheriff's House in the background, is where the ghost of Giles Corey is said to appear before an impending disaster.

The crushing of Giles Corey, 1692, as depicted at Salem's Witch Museum. The old man's dying words were a curse on the Sheriff and on Salem.
Photo courtesy Salem Witch Museum.

II
In Wake of Salem Witches

There is an old ballad, popular as a children's song in Salem some two centuries ago, that tells the story of the crotchety old wizard Giles Corey, who was accused of witchcraft at age eighty in 1692. It goes as follows:

> *"'Giles Corey,' said the Magistrate, 'What art thou here to plead, To these that now accuse thy soul of crimes and horrid deed?' Giles Corey, he said not a word, no single word spoke he. 'Giles Corey', said the Magistrate, 'We'll press it out of thee.' They got them a heavy beam. They laid it on his breast; They loaded it with heavy stones, And hard upon him prest. 'More weight!' now said the wretched man; 'More weight!' again he cried; And he did no confession make, but wickedly he dyed."*

The crushing of Giles Corey was probably the most tragic and brutal murder in the name of justice ever performed in America and certainly the most terrible in New England. Prior to his crushing, his wife Martha was accused and imprisoned as a Salem Witch during the winter of '92. Giles pleaded with the Sheriff and Magistrate that he be allowed to stay in the dank dungeon beneath the jail with her, but they refused him. It wasn't long, however, before the vicious teenaged girls of Salem Village accused him of witchcraft as well. Standing before the court, the courageous old man would not answer any questions. When asked how he pleaded, guilty or not guilty, he remained mute. By not pleading one way or the other, English law dictated that a person could not be tried, but the penalty for standing mute was slow crushing under weights, until a plea was forthcoming or the person died.

Many believed that Giles remained silent because otherwise, by law, the Sheriff could confiscate all his goods and property. The High Sheriff of Essex County, George Corwin, young nephew of Magistrate Jonathan Corwin, had already stripped the homes of the many accused of witchcraft. Oddly enough, those who pleaded not-guilty were condemned, and those who said they were guilty of witchcraft, were reprieved—but still languished in jail. Giles was a stubborn, fiery man, who realized he would not get a fair trial. His silence was also his way of showing contempt for the accusing girls, the pompous Magistrates, and the thieving Sheriff.

On Monday, September 19, 1692, the Sheriff and his deputies led Giles Corey stripped naked to a pit in the open field beside the Witch Jail. He was made to lie down in the pit, then six men lifted heavy stones, placing them one

19

by one on a door that had been laid over his stomach and chest. Giles Corey did not cry out in pain, which perplexed Sheriff Corwin, whose duty it was to squeeze a confession from him.

"Do you confess?" the Sheriff cried over and over again. More rocks were piled onto him, and Sheriff Corwin, from time to time, would stand on the boulders to stare down menacingly at Corey's bulging eyes.

"In the crushing, Giles Corey's tongue was pressed out of his mouth," wrote Robert Calef, a witness to the torture, *"and the Sheriff, with his cane, forced it in again."*

Finally, just before he expired, Corey cried out, *"Damn you Sheriff! I curse you and Salem!"*

Every High Sheriff of Essex County it seems, from the cruel George Corwin to myself, elected to the post 280 years later, has suffered in some way from Giles Corey's Curse. Sheriff Corwin was so disliked by the people of Salem, that when he died of a heart attack in 1696, his family didn't dare bury him in the cemetery for fear he'd be dug up and his body torn limb from limb. He was instead temporarily buried in the basement of his own home, a place today known as the Joshua Ward House, and considered quite haunted. From all the information that has been made available to me, it seems that all the High Sheriffs of Essex County since Corwin, headquartered at the Salem Jail located in the field where Giles Corey was crushed to death, died in office from heart attack, or were forced to retire because of heart conditions or blood ailments. The High Sheriff, before I took office some eighteen years ago, still suffers from a blood ailment that caused him to retire; and his father, the Sheriff before him, died of a heart attack in office. When I was forced to retire in 1978, it was after suffering a heart-attack, stroke, and undergoing many blood transfusions for a rare blood disease. Were we all victims, I wonder, of Giles Corey's curse?

"Tradition was long current in Salem," wrote Salem's noted author Nathaniel Hawthorne, *"that at stated periods, the ghost of Giles Corey, the wizard, appeared on the spot where he had suffered, as the precursor of some calamity that was impending over the community, which the apparition came to announce."*

Giles not only cursed the Sheriff with his dying breath, but Salem as well, and although the small city of 40,000 residents has thrived in the past 300 years, she has suffered periodic major setbacks. When my father was a boy of fourteen, there was an increase of sightings of the forlorn and ghastly ghost of Giles Corey at and near the Howard Street Burying-Ground, which backs up to the Old Salem Jail and the Sheriff's residence. *"People were saying that they saw this pitiful creature all bent over, wringing its bony hands as it floated among the old gravestones,"* my father told me. *"So, me and Ben Getchell stayed in the cemetery one night on a dare. At first it was fun and Ben and I laughed a lot,"* said Dad, *"but then it got cold and damp and real spooky. About Midnight Ben screamed. He saw a humanlike grey cloud sweeping across the graveyard coming toward us. I had fallen asleep, but I didn't even turn to look at the ghost of Giles Corey, I just got up and ran as fast as I could out of the cemetery and up Howard Street, with Ben on my heels, howling all the way. We must have woken up the whole neighborhood that night,"* laughed Dad , *"I never did see the ghost, and we lost the bet to boot!"*

Others, however, swore that they did see the ghost in 1914, and it was shortly thereafter that Salem suffered her greatest disaster. The Great-Fire ironically started at Gallows Hill, where 19 witches were hanged, including Giles Corey's wife, executed three days after he was crushed to death. The wind whipped the flames from housetop to housetop into the center of the city and then to the seacoast, but by some weird twist of fate, it leapt over and did not even singe any of the houses in the historic districts; yet, almost one-third of the city was destroyed. Is it, as Nat Hawthorne says, *"the ghost of the wizard appears as a precursor of some calamity impending over the community?"* Or were the increase in sightings before the Great Salem Fire only a coincidence?

The old Salem Jail and the Sheriff's House behind the cemetery, both built during the War of 1812, are vacant today, but they were in constant operation for 180 years. The Old Witch Jail of 1692, had been torn down to make way for them. Beneath the Witch Jail, was the dungeon where those awaiting the hangman were kept, and part of this dungeon was uncovered in 1957, when the New England Telephone Company began excavation across the street from the Sheriff's House to build the foundation for its new headquarters. Retrieved from the old dungeon were a few oak beams, only two of which are on display today, one at the Essex Institute and the other at the Witch Dungeon Museum in Salem.

* * * * * * * * * *

It was soon after I retired as Sheriff of the county that I found myself in the newly created Witch Dungeon Museum with glue, clay and some fifty mannequins, sculpturing the characters, including Giles Corey, of the 1692 witch hysteria. I had to work many nights in the damp cellar on Lynde Street, moulding the gloomy faces of the accusers and the victims, and I often felt chilled, not just from the cold and dampness, but sometimes from the ugliness of the characters I was creating.

The opening of the Witch Dungeon Museum with live re-enactments of the witch trials and a tour of the recreated dungeon, was slated for Friday the thirteenth, September 1979. That morning, only moments before the doors were about to open to the public, my nephew and namesake, Bob Cahill, fell from a thirty-foot ladder in front of the performing stage and into the pews, smashing the bones in his arm to tiny splinters. He wears an iron-plate in that arm to this day, and needless to say, the Witch Dungeon didn't open on that Friday the thirteenth. Many accidents and delaying incidents plagued the opening of the Witch Dungeon until Halloween, and on that day, another baffling mystery haunted the place.

The actresses who performed the trial of Sarah Good on stage, thirteen times a day, complained to the manger that amongst the clay characters I produced in the Dungeon below, they were encountering a monkish ghost. A few patrons also reported seeing what looked like a friar or monk in hooded tan robe in the maze of narrow corridors. The six actresses started calling the ghost, *"The Minister,"* which surprised me somewhat, since they were unaware that the building that the museum was now in, was once a church. The Minister was spotted so often, however, that the actresses finally refused to enter the Dungeon alone, which was part of their duties once they performed on stage. Jim Hurrell, one of the owners of the museum, scoffed at their sightings and talked to the girls one at a time in an attempt to allay these fears. A couple of the girls, including my niece Cheryl, were adamant. They had seen, if only but for a quick side-glance, the cloudy spirit of a hooded man in a robe, looking much like an ancient monk. He strolled the Dungeon, sometimes near the *"Crushing Scene of Giles Corey,"* and sometimes at a straw-roofed house that stands near the *"Scene of the Gallows Hill Hanging."* My red-headed, freckle-faced friend, Jim Hurrell, would almost explode with anger. *"There are no ghosts down there!"* he shouted. *"Bob and I built the place and we worked down there many a night into the wee hours. If there were ghosts down there, we would have seen them, and there were no ghosts—Now, go back to work and forget all that baloney!"*

Jimmy's heated speeches were effective, or at least I thought so, but the girls were still timid about going down into the dark Dungeon. My niece, Cheryl, kept insisting to me that what she and the girls saw was a real ghost, and that Jimmy Hurrell and the other owners should be more sympathetic to their fears. Cheryl has always had a wonderful imagination, so I didn't take her reports of a ghost too seriously either, although they did remind me of the chills I often had experienced working on the mannequins late into the night in the Dungeon.

It was early on Sunday morning that Cheryl called me. *"None of the actresses will go down into the Dungeon,"* she announced. All the girls refused to escort visitors through the maze of corridors, because of the ghost. Although close to hysterics, Cheryl explained over the phone as best she could. In the house with the straw roof near the Hanging Scene, was a hooded devil sitting in a rocking chair, holding a book in his lap. Jim Hurrell had built this one room house and I had decorated the interior with a bookcase, bureau, butter-churn, mirror and other bric-a-brac. *"The rocking chair keeps moving,"* said Cheryl, *"and the devil is moaning like some demon."*

22

"*It's all fake*," I said to Cheryl, trying to keep my composure. "*The devil is a dummy with a mask on, and nothing can move in that house, because no one can get inside it.*"

Jim and I had constructed the one-room house with only one way in and that was a crawl-space, known only to Jim and I, which led to the fireplace but was covered by a black curtain. The only way in was to lift the curtain and crawl through the fake fireplace. The appearance of fire in the fireplace was just a red light which provided a continuous dim glow of hot coals, and gave the devil sitting in the rocker an eerie look. There were two windows looking in on this scene from the corridor: one showing just a hooded figure sitting in the chair; but the other window gave the visitor a face-to-face peek at the hideous mask under the hood—the devil himself holding his book filled with the signatures of witches who had sold their souls to him. A nice little horrific scene, but surely not one to drive customers and employees away. "*Some of the tourists ran outside when they saw the devil move, Uncle Bob, and you wouldn't believe the sounds coming out of the devil's mouth.*"

"*Come on Cheryl, someone's got to be kidding.*"

"*No Uncle Bob, it's all very serious,*" she replied, her voice quivering. "*None of the girls will go down there again, and neither will I, so you'd better get down here, quick!*"

I live less than a mile away from the Witch Dungeon, but I was furious that my Sunday morning was disturbed by a bunch of over-sensitive, paranoid girls who couldn't keep their wits about them. When I walked inside the museum I was surrounded by costumed young ladies, all babbling at once in my ear. It was obvious that they were frightened, as were the few potential customers who were listening with their mouths ajar.

"*These are the same fears and hallucinations that caused the witch hysteria of 1692,*" I shouted at the girls. I explained to them that no one could be moving the rocking chair inside the room because no one could get in the room, which only heightened their hysteria and their belief that a ghost was moving the devil and his chair, and it was a ghost who was moaning and screeching.

"*It's like all the clay figures you made down there that are chained to the walls, are coming to life,*" said a wide-eyed Cheryl to me. They watched from the stairwell as I ventured down into the Dungeon. I acted angry and disgusted, but I also felt a bit weak-kneed as I entered this place of suffering and torture which I had re-created. Was this, I wondered, the penalty I must pay for making these poor victims relive their hell of 1692?

I gingerly walked through the narrow corridors, with cells on either side and my own clay creations staring at me through the bars as I passed. It's the first time I realized how really creepy the place was. When I came to Salem Village

An accused witch frightens accuser, actress Cheryl Cahill, in the live re-enactment of the trial of Sarah Good, performed many times each day at the Witch Dungeon Museum in Salem. Cheryl was one of the actresses who refused to escort tourists into the Dungeon because of sightings of the hooded monk ghost. The ghost was later captured. Photo below is the Witch Dungeon Museum, Salem, Massachusetts.

and the Hanging Scene, I peered through one of the two diamond-paned windows of the straw-roofed house. Everything looked fine in the dimly lit room: the devil was sitting silently in his rocking chair with the book on his lap; the surrounding furniture was in place; and the fire-place hearth provided its warm glow. I heard no sounds and I saw no change inside the room. I walked upstairs and announced to the girls that they were letting their imaginations run wild.

"No one likes a good ghost story like I do," I told them, *"and I've even gone looking for ghosts from time to time, but I assure you, there are no ghosts down there. So please, open the doors and get back to work!"* Some of girls looked a little embarrassed and admitted that they might have over-reacted, but my niece, Cheryl, refused to admit that it was nothing.

"I saw the rocking chair rock," she insisted, *"and I heard the devil cry out, and the tourists I was with heard it and saw it too!"* I could have strangled her. I finally got her to agree to tour visitors through the Dungeon with two tour guides instead of one, and said that if there were any more strange incidents to call me at home, where I intended to be all day.

Early that afternoon, Jim Hurrell and his family came to visit me, and they had just settled in when the phone rang. *"You've got to get down here right away,"* Cheryl screamed, *"the devil is rocking all over the room. Tourists are leaving this place in panic and all the actresses are ready to leave too. Get down here right now, or we'll have to close up. I'm not going to stay in this place,"* she shouted in near panic. *"If you're not here in five minutes, I'm out of here."*

I repeated to Jim what Cheryl said as we drove to the Dungeon. *"Ridiculous,"* Jim kept saying over and over again, *"Ridiculous!"* Cheryl and the other actresses were on the sidewalk when we pulled up to the building, and they started jabbering all at once. One of the girls actually was in tears. They had all seen the chair with the devil in it rocking violently back and forth, with such intensity that the large book he was holding had fallen on the floor. Two of the girls said that they saw the hooded monk standing behind the chair rocking it. Another had heard the monk laughing, a deep, hideous, mocking laugh.

Jim threw up his hands and fended them off as he headed into the museum, calling them all *"a bunch of wimps."* Bravely he headed down the stairs to the Dungeon and the ghost with me at his heels. As we scurried by dummies in the stocks and pillories and the old familiar faces of those behind bars, Jim looked at me and smiled. *"This place is kind of creepy though, ain't it?"* Jim looked in one of the house windows at the dimly lit room as I looked in the other window. *"I see nothing wrong,"* he said.

But I did! I could see that the rocking chair had moved a least a foot since I was there that morning. *"You're nuts too,"* said Jimmy when I told him that the devil and his chair had moved. *"No one knows how to get into that room but you* and me," said Jim, "and who'd want to crawl all the way through that dusty tunnel to get in there anyway, unless they had to replace a burnt-out bulb or something like that." I agreed, but something was obviously moving the chair and frightening the girls. "Well, you'll just have to go in there and see," said Jim. I didn't respond.

About two doors down from the straw-roofed house, was the mannequin of an old woman sweeping out a doorway. I got down on my hands and knees and crawled behind her, through a myriad of wires and down about ten feet between black wall panels to the cloth that hung behind as a back-drop to the plaster-of-paris fireplace. Cobwebs kept brushing my face, so I knew that no one had been through this passageway recently. I was ready to lift the black curtain, when a gutteral, ear-piercing screech came from the room that I was just about to enter. Although the inhuman sound gave me chills, I immediately concluded it came from Jimmy Hurrell, who was supposedly staring into the room through one of the windows.

"Cut it out, Jimmy!" I shouted, trying to sound perturbed.

"That wasn't me that made that sound," said Jimmy. "I thought it was you!"

I could tell from the tone and direction of his voice that it wasn't Jimmy who had emitted the bone-chilling scream. I started to quickly back out of the passageway, still on my hands and knees.

"What the hell is it?" I shouted at Jim as I crawled backwards.

"I don't see anything," said Jim.

Once again came the sound, more like the wailing of a child, and it frightened me so that I started feeling sick. I heard Jim curse and realized that he was frightened too.

"Don't you run on me, Hurrell," I shouted. "Don't you leave me in here alone!" My legs felt wobbly and weak as I tried to squeeze under the mannequin's broom.

"Hold it, hold it!" shouted Jimmy, his hands cupped to the diamond panes of glass. "I see it, I see it!"

Now I really felt faint—Jimmy Hurrell was telling me he saw the ghost. "It's there, It's there!" he shouted, "Under the bureau!"

I rolled out into the corridor, my hair and clothes covered with dust and cobwebs, and I ran to the other window of the house. "What is it?" I shouted at Jim.

"Look, Look!" he said, in almost a whisper, not taking his face nor his cupped hands from the other window.

At first I saw nothing unusual, but then the spirit of the haunted room, the creature with the chilling shrill voice of a demon, made its appearance. Slowly and stealthily it moved from the shadows into the dim light. It went to the rocking chair and leapt onto the devil's lap. There, it settled in and began purring. A cat!

"I can't believe it," said Jimmy. *"How did it get in there?"*

I looked up and saw that inside the room, part of the false ceiling had fallen in. It must have found a way into the museum and crawled up above the dungeon structures built by Jimmy and then had obviously fallen into the room. It could find no way out of the room, but was comforted in the rocking chair on the devil's lap. When someone noisily came down the corridor, it jumped off the devil's lap which got the chair moving and it hid in the shadows under the bureau. When anyone looked into the room, all they saw was the devil rocking back and forth. I crawled back in and fetched the cat from the lap of the devil. It belonged to a neighbor and had been missing for four days, thus the reason for the occasional fiendish yowl—it was thirsty and hungry. The actresses were, of course, relieved, and Jimmy Hurrell strutted around the museum with an *"I told you so,"* air about him all day.

Peace in the dungeon was short-lived however, for Cheryl and a few of the other girls started seeing the monk again while escorting tourists down below, and especially when they had to shut off the lights at day's end. He appears now more frequently near the Crushing Scene, they tell me, and I'm not one to so easily dispel their sightings anymore, for, after all, their ghost in the rocking chair proved to be real.

* * * * * * * * * *

One day shortly after the cat episode in the dungeon, a real monk came to visit me about ghosts. His name was Brian and he was a Franciscan lay-monk. He had read my book *"New England Ghostly Haunts,"* published by Chandler-Smith in 1983, and was especially anxious to learn more about the hauntings at Salem's Joshua Ward House. This is a handsome brick mansion built in the mid 18th century by wealthy merchant Joshua Ward, on the foundation of Sheriff George Corwin's home and where he was initially buried in 1696. George Washington slept on the second floor of the house in 1789, but otherwise the history of the house was uneventful until 1981. It was then that Richard Carlson bought the building for his expanding real estate business. It was not too long after Carlson and his bevy of employees moved into the old house that they realized it was haunted, not by the ghost of Sheriff Corwin, but by a witch-like spirit who wasn't too shy about letting people know she was haunting the place.

"I take infra-red photographs of ghosts," said Brian-the-monk, *"and I want to spend the night in the house with you to capture the ghost on film."*

"The ghost has already been captured on film," I told him. Realtor Dale Lewinski, using a Polaroid camera, was taking head and shoulder shots of all the Carlson employees working in the house to be displayed on a door wreath at

Christmas time. As she took Lorraine St. Pierre's photo, the ghost stepped in and the Polaroid captured the ghost rather than Lorraine on film. Lorraine was frightened, even slightly embarrassed about it, but she turned the photo over to me for publication.

"I'd like to get the ghost on infra-red film," said Brian-the-monk.

"I don't think I want to spend a night in the Joshua Ward House," I replied. *"This seems like one truly malicious ghost to me, and I'm not anxious to get her dander up."*

I had interviewed all the employees at Carlson, and some of the women were really frightened. Julie Tache, who was first to contact me, said, *"even though I lock my office door every night, when I open up in the morning, my lamp-shade or my waste basket is tipped upside down, or all my desk items are scattered across the room and books are on the floor, pulled out of the bookcase. The crowning blow was when I arrived one morning to find the two brass candle holders on my fireplace mantle turned upside down and the two candles were on the floor, one reshaped into a perfect 's', and the other bent like a boomerang. There was no logical way this could have happened unless the room got so hot during the night that the candles wilted."*

Julie moved out of her second-floor office for one on the first floor, but the harrassment by unseen hands continued and she eventually moved out altogether. Julie also told me that the fire alarm sounded at least sixty times late at night during the two years she was working in the house, and either she or Dick Carlson was called out in the middle of the night, but when she was called out, the alarm would go off by itself, but as Julie stated, *"when Dick had to come to the house, the ghost would make him come into the house and shut off the alarm with his key."* It soon became obvious that the ghost had a crush on Dick.

Dick's office on the second floor backs up to the room George Washington slept in. In this room there is a large closet where Dick keeps all his land graphs, floor plans, and zoning maps rolled up and stuffed into cubby-holes. One day while in his office with employee Virginia Kohler discussing a house sale, the phone rang. The man on the line asked Dick for a specific plan of property in Marblehead, which Dick said he had, but it would take him awhile to locate the plan in his closet. *"At that moment before Virginia's and my eyes,"* said Dick Carlson, *"a rolled up plan came floating out of the closet, hit the floor and spread itself out before my desk—it was the plan that the guy on the other end of the phone was looking for."*

"So you see," I explained to Brian-the-monk, *"I have no doubt that the Joshua Ward House is haunted, and I therefore have no reason to go there to be frightened out of my wits...that would only be looking for trouble."*

Brian was persistent, possibly in keeping with his holy order, but I was just as adamant. If he wished to stay there the night alone, I would call Dick Carlson to see if he could stay. *"I'm sure that they have a vacant room you can use,"* I joked, but the monk was serious—ghosts were not a joking matter to him. It was like my new-found friend was on some sort of crusade. He didn't seem to like ghosts much, whereas, I was usually either amused or frightened to near death by them. They always intrigued me, which kept me coming back for more information and inevitably more punishment. Nevertheless, I was determined not to spend a night in the Joshua Ward House.

Even my own sister-in-law, Cheryl's mother, Barbara Cahill, had seen the ghost of the wicked witch of the Joshua Ward House, and Barb wasn't the type to see things that weren't there. *"I was sitting in the front office of the first floor, waiting for Sherry Kerr to help me find an apartment,"* Barb told me. *"I immediately noticed a strange looking woman sitting in a wingback chair across the hall in another office. The woman's skin didn't look like flesh, but was almost transparent like glass. She looked like a mannequin, just staring into space, and during the few minutes I was waiting for Sherry to get off the phone, the woman didn't move a muscle. Although other people were around, no one paid any attention to her. It was as if I was the only one who could see her. She looked really weird, with frizzled hair and wearing a long grey coat. She gave me a very eerie feeling, but then Sherry got off the phone and I turned away, never looking back into that room. I thought about that woman for days afterward,"* said Barbara, *"still wondering if she was a real person or not."* This all happened prior to Barbara's hearing that the house was haunted and before the Polaroid of the ghost was taken. Her description of the woman she saw fit the photograph of the ghost perfectly and the photo was taken only inches from where Barb's strange woman had been sitting, right near the front door of the house.

My stories didn't dissuade Brian-the-monk. He wanted to meet this ghost. Here was a real ghost-buster, I concluded. He carried infra-red binoculars—which he paid a small fortune for—purchased from an Israeli Army Captain, and his camera was filled with infra-red film. He had rosary beads, holy water and he wore a thick wooden cross chained to his neck—these were his weapons. The infra-red, so Brian explained to me, would reveal all energy which is warmth, and spirits are energy, which meant they could be photographed, and the religious objects would, he hoped, protect him from any evil energy. I got him his entry into the haunted house through Dick Carlson, and as I watched this hawk-nosed, cherub-like friar leave my house, I got the vivid impression of a young medieval knight heading out to slay the dragon. It was two days later that I got a report back from Brian on what happened that evening:

"John, the maintenance man, let me in and I went through every room snapping my pictures," he told me, *"the most significant thing that happened to me was when I climbed the stairs to the second floor and entered the room on*

the right (the one Washington slept in). In that room all the lights were out and upon entering it my throat immediately tightened up, and it was like someone was choking me. I was being strangled but I didn't feel any hands around my throat. Yet I felt my throat close up. I shouted to John, the maintenance man, that I was choking to death. He thought I was kidding at first, but then he saw that I wasn't getting any air. However, the moment I got outside of that room and in the hallway again, all strangling symptoms left me."

Brian-the-monk left the Joshua Ward House shortly thereafter, as did John Gagnon, the maintenance man, who has never worked in the house after dark since the evening when he was alone in the house and he was grabbed from behind on the stairway by unseen hands. *"I felt hands on my shoulders weighing me down,"* said John.

So Brian-the-monk didn't spend the night, and although he took a lot of photos with infra-red film, he didn't get pictures of the ghost. He got many photos with white blobs on them that he thought might be spirits, but what I thought were white blobs. More important than his photos, however, was his experience of being strangled. Others, unbeknownst to Brian, had told me that they had a similar choking experience in that same room; Julie Tache for one, and one of Dick Carlson's relatives for another. Ironically, old Sheriff Corwin of Witch Hysteria Days, was known as *"The Strangler,"* because of his cruel method of torture used to gain confessions. John Proctor, who was eventually hanged as a wizard in Salem in 1692, revealed before he died that the Sheriff and his deputies tortured by strangulation the young innocent sons of accused witch Martha Carrier. *"The boys were tied neck and heels,"* said Proctor, *"til the blood was ready to come out their noses and eyes."*

Is it the Sheriff that haunts the old house, one wonders, practicing his strangulation techniques to this very day? Or might the hag-like creature seen and photographed by the front stairs in the house be the Sheriff's wife? We shall probably never know, but thanks to that ugly ghost, I have made a new friend with a hobby of hunting down spirits, and unlike the ghost in the Witch Dungeon, Brian is a real monk!

The Wicked Witch Ghost of the Joshua Ward House is captured on Polaroid film by Dale Lewinski while working for Carlson Realty. This ghost has been seen by others and has molested many who work in or visit the house. The Joshua Ward House of Salem (insert) is presently up for sale.

Newburyport's Frog Pond, with the old courthouse on the left, said to be the hub of a wheel of underground tunnels where spirits dwell. Below, Brian-the-monk stands in front of the keeper's house of the old Newburyport Jail complex, where the owner says there are no ghosts, but Brian insists there are.

III
Spirits of the Frog Pond

It is a lovely little pond located high on a hill overlooking downtown Newburyport and the mouth of the Merrimack River. Local kids fish here in the summer and skate here in the winter. In the spring, the croaking of the frogs is deafening. The massive, intricately designed bronze fountain that has been standing in the middle of the pond since 1891 had to be hauled away in 1988 for repairs—a hockey puck had knocked off the bill of the swan that spouts water from the top of the fountain. It had been called the Frog Pond from as far back as anyone could remember. A transfer of four acres of land from William Titcomb to Christopher Bartlett, recorded in the Ipswich Deed Book of 1651, reads *"in the field called the lower nine lotts, bounded by the highway neare the Frogg Pond on the south..."* and it was from then on known as Bartlett's Mall.

In 1804 the town and county voted unanimously *"in placing a new court house on land between Frog Pond and the mall,"* and the following year, it was recorded that, *"the new edifice designed by Bulfinch is an imposing structure with square brick columns or pillars in front and the figure of 'Justice' with evenly balanced scales, standing above the entrance."* Behind the courthouse, old town records reveal, *"about an acre of land on the south-westerly side of Frog Pond, now known as 'Old hill Burying Ground,' was enclosed with a board fence and set apart as a burial-place by the inhabitants in 1730."* It was soon after that Colonel Moses Titcomb, commander of the Newburyport battery, led his men to the successful capture of Louisburg; and again in 1755, when hostilities between France and England were renewed, Colonel Titcomb led his men into Canada. He was killed in the battle at Crown Point and returned in a box to be buried at Old Hill Burying Ground in land once owned by his great-grandfather.

To make the lovely loop complete, linking the old burial ground, the brick courthouse, the pond, and the 18th century mansions lining High Street, a stone jail was built *"with house and barn and a wall around same,"* in 1825 on the hill overlooking this typically New England scene. I was standing in front of that old stone jail on the beautiful spring morning the crane lifted the fountain from the pond for repairs, awaiting Brian-the-monk who had obtained permission from the girlfriend of the new owner of the jail to tour the premises. Brian assured me that the jail complex, including jail, house and barn, or carriage house as they now called it, was haunted, although the new owner of the complex, Chuck Griffin, thought the hauntings were *"a lot of hogwash."*

Strangely enough, some ten years earlier, I was in charge of the pretty little brick courthouse on Frog Pond, and I might have lived in the supposedly haunted jailhouse, if it hadn't been for a feisty and famous mayor of Newburyport named Bossy Gillis. Gillis, known as *"The Little Irish-Brawler,"* once owned a gas station in town, but the then mayor, Michael Cashman, wouldn't allow him to expand his business, so Bossy punched Cashman in the nose, and went to jail for it. After spending a few months behind bars at Salem Jail, Bossy decided to run against Cashman for Mayor, announcing his candidacy on the day he got out. Surprisingly, Bossy won. One of his first moves was to buy the Newburyport jail complex from the county, and to set up housekeeping for his mother in the jailhouse. The reason he did this, his political opponents declared, *"is that when he's sent to jail again, his mother will be right there to care for him."* Bossy died the month and year that I won my first political race as a Salem City Councillor, November, 1965. By that time, Bossy had run for Mayor 21 times and had won a few times–but he also lost more than a few times.

When I was elected the Sheriff of Essex County, the picturesque Newburyport Courthouse was under my jurisdiction. A terrorist group blew it up on Fourth of July eve in 1976. They blew up other things, too...an airliner sitting empty on the tarmac at Logan Airport, a post office, and another courthouse in Boston. But why this little antique court in Newburyport, I'll never know. The damage was quite extensive, but it was repaired, and trials are still held today within its hallowed halls.

It was after Brian showed up and we entered the fenced in jail yard that the new owner, Chuck Griffin, confronted us before we entered the old stone building. He called us *"terrorists."* He had a pencil-line smile on his face, but I knew he was serious. He spoke loudly to Brian.

"I just purchased this place for a good amount of money, and now my girlfriend is threatening to return to Iowa, and the workmen are almost frightened to death, afraid to go into the carriage-house basement or into the jail, only because you keep talking to them about ghosts."

"Your girlfriend said she was having nightmares since she arrived here," Brian told Griffin.

"It's no wonder, with all the talk of evil spirits. She's not used to this stuff. We're from Iowa. We don't have this kind of stuff in Iowa."

Brian looked frightened. He was now worried that Mr. Griffin wasn't going to let him take infra-red photos inside the jail. *"Your girlfriend said we could take photos in the jail,"* Brian said meekly.

"Photos of what? There's nothing in there...and there are no ghosts in there either, I just had the whole place sandblasted, drove all the spirits right out of there." He smiled, noting Brian's disappointed expression. *"Oh, all right, Go ahead,"* he said, scurrying off across the courtyard to the carriage house, *"but I don't want to hear anymore about ghosts, and I don't want you to talk to her*

34

about them either." Brian promised, then hurried on toward the jail with me at his heels.

We entered the square two storied building and I immediately felt the bone-chilling cold permeating off the granite—the place was freezing. There were two large black iron doors, one was the main entrance and the other was to close off a solitary confinement cell. The bars on the open windows were made of iron, too, but otherwise everything was stone. The old jail was made without a particle of wood, only granite and iron were used in its construction. Piles of sand and grit from the granite littered the stone floors from the recent sandblasting. There were only eight small cells within the building and each had a metal bunk in it, but there was no other furniture in the cells—no fireplace, no stove, no electricity, no running water. The opening to get into each cell was so narrow that I had to squeeze in sideways to enter. The old Salem Jail, where I was Master and Keeper for over four years, was built in 1811, and even though the inmates had to relieve themselves in buckets, there was heat and electricity and one didn't have to squeeze into the cells. The Newburyport Jail, however, closed down for lack of funds in 1918; whereas, the antiquated Salem Jail remained open until 1991, operating continuously for 180 years.

"This place is definitely haunted," said Brian as he breezed in and out of each cell snapping infra-red photos. *"There are two women ghosts in the cell on the second floor, facing the house."*

I went up there to look around. It looked like all the other cells, except that the windows of the house, where the keepers of the jail and Bossy Gillis' mother once lived, were only a few feet away. The window facing the supposed haunted cell was shuttered, so that you couldn't look into the house from the jail.

"That's the main bedroom in the house," Brian informed me, *"and its where Jeremiah, the previous tenant, and his girlfriend slept. The reason they moved out of the house is because of the ghosts in this cell who watched over them each night. It's also the reason why the window shutters on just that window are closed and locked tight."*

There was only a small narrow courtyard between the house and jail, and I noticed that the black shutters on all the other windows were open and folded back against the granite of the squat little house.

"Jeremiah had nightmares every night since he moved into the house," said Brian, dancing around me, snapping photos into the cold air, his intent being to catch some unsuspecting ghost on the infra-red film. *"He told me that he heard a humming noise coming from the jail, and his girlfriend, who lived in the house with him, heard it too. They used to leave the shutters open, and she felt drawn to the window each night. She'd look across the few feet into the jail cell and see shadows moving. Many a night he'd wake up from his nightmares in a cold sweat, and when he looked out the window, he'd get an eerie feeling, so he kept the shutters closed. That's when the humming sound got louder and more*

distinctive. It sounded like soft singing of little girls or women, and then he heard the whisperings of two females. Jeremiah went to Yale Divinity School, so he's up on demonic possession, and that's just what these ghostly females in the jail wanted—they wanted to possess his girlfriend, he concluded. So, he packed his bag and hers, and he moved out . He still lives in Newburyport, and he says his girl sometimes still hears the humming sounds and that she's vexed by it."

"Well, I'm certainly getting chills in here," I told Brian, *"but I think it's from the wind whistling through these windows. How anyone locked up in here could survive a winter is beyond me."*

"Where do you feel the chill?" asked Brian, his camera poised.

"In the back of the neck," I replied.

Brian snapped a picture and we were quickly out of there, but strangely, when that photo was developed, it showed a blurry figure or two standing next to the barred window. There was nothing else in that cell, nothing but bare walls and not a stick of furniture, when I was in there, yet....Staring closely at the blurs in the photo, they looked to me like one person sitting, cradling another in a blanket, with only the head and hands exposed. Was I seeing things, imagining something was there that wasn't? I don't know, but I do know that nothing was in that cell when Brian took the photo, or at least, nothing that I could see.

"Who else has seen or heard these ghosts?" I asked Brian.

"Two of the carpenters who are working here, fixing up the house, jail and carriage house. Griffin is attempting to restore everything before it falls into disrepair. One is an Irish lad named Dermot Bray. He was in the jail and heard moaning and screaming."

"I'm of Irish descent myself," I told Brian, *"and we Irish are very superstitious....It was probably some of his fellow workers just fooling around, knowing he was susceptible to such things."*

"I don't think so," said Brian, *"but I'll let you talk to the other workman, Rick Seagale, and you can come to your own conclusions."*

I talked to Rick later that day: *"I was in the basement of the carriage house,"* said Rick, *"all alone down there, or at least I thought I was."*

Rick struck me as a serious minded, hard-working young man, and his voice quivered as he told me his story, so I knew he was reliving his experience as he told it.

"All of a sudden it seemed to get smoky down there, like there was a fog or something. I looked up and saw two glowing golden lines in the air, like light hairs, or a cobweb floating only about four feet in front of me. I thought it was a web of dust from the sandblaster at first, but then it transformed into the likeness of a woman, She was facing left and away from me, looking into the stone wall which was only some ten feet away. Her sandy-colored hair was down to her shoulders and looped back up to a bun. She wore a tight fitting skirt that flared

at the hips. The sleeves were puffy, but I couldn't see her lower body because of piles of boxes between her and me. As I recall it now, I should have realized that she couldn't fit in that space. The background seemed 100 feet and beyond, like there were buildings behind her. I moved to my left and tried to better focus my eyes. At first I thought she was a real woman, but then I realized the perspective was all off. When I waved my hand in front of my face, the air seemed much colder. She began moving off and getting smaller, like she was going through a doorway to some other space. Her image was quite clear and real to me. I wasn't horror-stricken, but I felt very uncomfortable and I feared that she might turn and face me. I don't know why, but I'm glad I didn't see her face. Before this happened to me, I didn't know that this place had a history of sightings, so it was all a big surprise for me. She gradually faded away into the wall, and while this was happening, it seemed like the wall was going away from the house. Chuck Griffin, of course, wasn't too happy to hear of my living nightmare in his newly acquired property. The image appeared for only about twenty seconds, but it was enough to scare the hell out of me, and I told Chuck that I won't work in the basement ever again".

Rick was obviously sincere and I didn't doubt a word he said. What intrigued me most was that this spirit appeared to him underground. It seems that many of the hauntings throughout the years in the vicinity of the Frog Pond have been beneath the earth's surface. And it also surprised me that all the ghosts hanging around the jail complex are women. A jail, I would think, should conjure up male spirits.

Researching the jail at the nearby Newburyport Library, hoping to find out who the ghosts might be, I discovered that 23,028 persons served time in the jail over a period of 93 years—most for menial crimes—and 99% of them were men. There was one cell set aside for women inmates, but the old records didn't indicate which cell, so I will assume it was the rear-right cell on the second floor, facing the bedroom in the house. Two women sharing that small cell would not be unusual. A newspaper account of *"the new gaol"* in 1825 described it as *"light and airy."* What an understatement that was! Revolutionary War General Marquis de Lafayette laid the jail's cornerstone, which adds a tad of distinction to the old place.

If I were to choose an inmate of the Newburyport Jail to come back as a permanent guest to haunt the place, it would be Luther French. He's the only person I've ever heard of who spent most of his life in jail when he didn't have to. The local police and the county sheriff asked him to leave the jail many times, but he wouldn't. When the Master and Keeper of the jail tried to force him out, he locked himself in. He remained in jail for over 34 years, yet he was convicted to serve only six.

Luther French's crime was love. He loved the daughter of the minister of the

The Newburyport Jail, built in 1825, closed in 1918. Brian-the-monk believes that it is haunted by two female ghosts. Looking through the bars across the small courtyard stands the carriage house, where carpenter Rick Seagale encountered a frightening underground ghost.

Top is the infra-red photo taken by Brian-the-monk inside an empty Newburyport jail cell, showing what appears to be a white figure or figures. On closer inspection it looks like a woman cradling an old bearded man, or is it just the movement of the wind coming through the barred window? This cell was empty and recently sandblasted when the photo was taken.

Below, Author Bob Cahill stands before the much maligned Pierce Tomb, where Newburyport teenagers performed macabre rituals with mummified corpses. The same tomb, shown in the photo right, is located at Old Burying Ground, just above the Frog Pond and near the jail, where ghosts have often been seen.

Colonel Moses Titcomb of Newburyport, Commander of artillery at Crown Point in 1775, returned home in a box and was buried at Old Hill Burying Ground, which was once land owned by his ancestors. At the Titcomb family plot, not far from the Pierce Tomb, Brian-the-monk caught the Colonel's ghost on infra-red film just leaving his gravestone. Only his head is visible on the stone, left of center. It looks like the Colonel hasn't changed much in appearance in 240 years.

Episcopal Church, Miss Lucy Morse. The Reverend Morse didn't love Luther, and he told him to stay away from his teenaged daughter. Luther kept sneaking back to see Lucy, so the reverend not only kicked the boy out of his house but out of the church as well. Luther threatened to shoot the minister, so he was arrested. Reverend Morse suggested to the police that Luther's love was insanity, so Luther was sent to the asylum first. The experts considered him sane, so he was tried for attempted murder, found guilty, and sent to Newburyport Jail for six years.

When it came time for his release in 1840, Luther refused to leave. There was no law on the books that forced a person to leave the jail when his sentence was up, so the sheriff allowed him to stay, thinking that this was only a temporary reluctance. After two years, the jail keeper insisted that Luther leave, but he again refused, and he wouldn't even step outside the jail for fear a guard would pounce on him and throw him out onto the street. Living in this damp, dingy and freezing cold cell for 34 years, Luther contracted pneumonia on December 2, 1868, and was carried out into *"the cold, cruel world,"* as he called it, to the hospital and thence to the Alms House, where he soon died. I can't think of a more appropriate ghost to haunt the Newburyport Jailhouse than Luther French. Even sandblasting wouldn't force his spirit to leave. I wonder, however, if the ghost Rick Seagale saw might not be that of Miss Lucy Morse, her penance in afterlife being constant visitations to the jail for a life misspent in rejected love.

When I talked to Rick about his terrible vision in the basement of the carriage house, I asked him in which direction this spirit was traveling through the wall. He indicated that she was heading southeast, which would be toward Burying Hill, or *"Old Hill Burying Ground,"* as they called it in the 1700s. This was where Brian-the monk himself had seen two ghosts, a man and a woman, in the recent past during a nightly vigil, using his infra-red binoculars. *"I watched them leave a tomb,"* Brian informed me, *"and walk to the rock wall that faces the street overlooking the Frog Pond. There was nothing spectacular about them. I took photos, but they came out as blurs on the infra-red film. They seemed to walk through the stone wall and then return to the tomb."*

This was the "Pierce" tomb, where in February of 1985, a macabre and grisly incident was revealed in the local newspapers. Ten teenagers had broken into the tomb, removed three mummified corpses from their coffins, poured beer and wine down their throats, performed a few more bizarre rituals, and generally used the tomb as a clubhouse for three weeks, until the caretaker discovered that the tomb had been broken into. The police and an undertaker were notified. The undertaker had to shroud and redress the corpses and place them back in their coffins. All in the tomb were members of the Pierce family, one woman and six men, the earliest being entombed in 1838. One was a drowning victim whose body was shipped up to Newburyport from New Jersey for burial.

41

The Newburyport News ran a front page appeal for the boys to come forward and turn themselves in to the police—it was announced that three of the people in the tomb had died of dangerous contagious diseases, which the vandals could have easily contracted. They showed up piecemeal at police headquarters and confessed, then they were rushed off to the hospital.

None of the boys were diseased, but surely something was wrong with them for uncovering and mistreating these corpses. They did it, apparently, just for a lark, and were unaware that boys their age had performed the same gruesome act back in 1925 to the very same corpses in the same Pierce tomb. They had dug an opening behind the tomb, broke through and dropped into the tomb on ropes. They then unraveled the brown shrouds that the bodies were wrapped in, and abused the mummified corpses by poking them with sticks. They sat the bodies up in their coffins to join them in macabre candlelight club meetings, and they began wearing the clothes of the corpses. That's how they were discovered. They were seen marching around the Frog Pond wearing 19th century shoes, pants, shirts and jackets, and their antics were reported to the police. They were arrested, confessed their disgusting deed, and the clothes were returned to the tomb.

Why, one wonders, is such mischief directed towards the Pierces? What draws teenagers to that particular tomb and entices them to perform such dastardly deeds? Brian-the-monk believes evil forces are at work all around the Frog Pond, it being like the hub of a great wheel, its spokes being under-ground tunnels that weave their way throughout downtown Newburyport, creating bedlam beneath the earth in a variety of places such as the jail and the burying ground. During one of his long nightly vigils at the cemetery above the pond, he sat amongst the gravestones and tombs of the Titcombs, the family that once owned the land around the Frog Pond and, since 1730, were planted in it when they died. Using his infra-red camera, Brian got a photo of Colonel Moses Titcomb's head, as he apparently was about to rise up from his grave to take a stroll around Burying Hill. If it isn't a head coming out of the gravestone, I don't know what it is, and it's a surprising likeness to the portrait of the Colonel that was painted in 1745. Brian says that the Colonel often sticks his head up from his grave on moonlit nights, *"just to see what's going on."*

"There's an intricate tunnel system under Burying Hill, through to High Street and down into town," said Brian. *"Most Newburyporters know about it and some have entrance to it from their homes. And all the locals I've talked to have concluded that its haunted. I explored the tunnel only recently,"* he informed me. *"A nurse, who lives on High Street, just east of the courthouse, has an entrance to the tunnel in her basement, which she uncovered during renovations. The tunnel frightened her and she thought she heard moans coming from it at night, so she called on me to explore it, which I did. With a light and*

my trusty camera, I walked in some 75-feet. The odor was bad in there, a smell that I couldn't begin to describe, yet it was dry and had a high brick ceiling and sturdy brick floor and walls. At the end of her tunnel, the system flared off into many other tunnels going in various directions, like spokes of a wheel, most seemed to be heading down into town. One that I entered went in for only five feet or so and was walled up with brick. It was like a little room, much like the Priest Holes found in the cellars in England used to hide outlawed members of the clergy. I noted that there were metal brackets high up on the walls that might have at one time held shelving, but otherwise, the tunnels were clean and empty."

There was a recent incident in downtown Newburyport, behind the shops on State Street, where an empty lot used for parking collapsed completely, and upon inspection it was discovered that the land had sunk into one of these brick tunnels. The newspaper called it a *"slave tunnel,"* and made the readers suppose that these underground brickworks were built to hide runaway slaves during the Underground Railroad days. Newburyport was a strong Abolitionist town prior to the Civil War, and the town's favorite son, William Lloyd Garrison, was the father of Abolitionism. But I believe the tunnels were constructed 100 years or more before the Civil War, probably well before the Revolutionary War. Other places like Salem, Boston and Newport, Rhode Island, have these oval brick tunnels too. Besides being mistaken for slave tunnels and old sewers, some believe they were built as hidden chambers to hide from hostile Indians, but they were probably constructed for smuggling. The heavy British import tax that finally drove Americans into battle with Mother England, was in force many years before the Revolution and was detested by all merchants. Smuggling goods in from vessels recently arrived from foreign lands to avoid the taxes was a popular pastime in the early 18th century, and what better way than to have a secret tunnel from the wharf to your home, where you could deliver goods unseen. It seems that all the towns that discovered such tunnels running under their streets are seacoasts towns, once active in foreign trade and privateering. It also seems strange that there is no record in old town histories of the tunnels being constructed. Why be so secretive about underground connecting links throughout the town, unless they were built for some devious purpose?

"It's almost as if Newburyport was duplicated underground as a city," says Brian, *"and nobody seems to know for sure why, but they are widely reputed to be haunted. In another old mansion on High Street, a few houses west of the courthouse, a young man, his wife and kids, just moved in, coming here from Maryland. In the basement, the man discovered an entrance to the tunnels. That family constantly heard cries, weeping and wailing coming from the tunnels. He cemented up the entrance with bricks and mortar, then put up a wooden wall in front of it. He's not sure if it caused the terrible sounds to stop, but he and his family can't hear them anymore."*

43

Reputed as the most haunted of these underground tunnels is the one that runs from the Frog Pond, with an entrance into the basement of the courthouse, straight down Green Street, past City Hall and the Garrison Inn and supposedly, on to the river, where the ancient entrance is now under-water. It is at the Garrison Inn some 100 yards from the pond, where seepage of undesirable spirits trickled in from the tunnel into the basement dining room while the Inn was being refurbished. Mark Lowler, the clerk at the Inn, says *"Margie Scanlon and Christie Gissel, waitress and bartender, first saw the ghosts of little ragged children, standing, as if begging, in the basement alcoves of brick, near the entrance to the dining room."* This portion of the basement was once part of the tunnel that led to the river. Begging children seemed appropriate spirits to me, since the Inn was originally *"elegant townhouses of brick"* in 1814, owned by philanthropist Moses Brown. He was often visited by beggars at his townhouse, they knowing that he would never refuse them. At his death in 1827, the Inn was transferred to his only relative, Sarah White Bannister, who supposedly also haunts the Inn. She died in 1880.

Sarah, so Brian informed me *"has been seen a number of times as of late, in a flowing white gown, almost always in front of a fireplace in the basement dining room, but one time before the fireplace in the reception area by the clerk, who was talking to a customer at the time. Sarah started dancing on a couch behind the guest, her gown blowing out behind her as if it was caught in the wind, but of course, there were no breezes blowing in the reception area. The clerk was frightened, but even more afraid to show it, for fear the customer would turn and see the ghost floating right behind him. She just kept the conversation going during the few moments the ghost did her dance, and then Sarah just disappeared."*

Receptionist Margaret Sullivan said that *"one evening a guest phoned down from his room and said that he was in his pajamas standing on his bed, for the other bed in the room was vibrating as if someone was shaking it. I couldn't leave the desk, so I invited him down, and he came down in his pajamas, had two double vodkas and returned to his room for a peaceful sleep. He also brought two more drinks with him to bed,"* added Margaret.

The new owner of the Inn, Janet Eisenberg, said a man *"just the other night complained that his bed was vibrating, but I couldn't figure out what it could be that made his bed move. I had never heard Margaret's story, so it didn't even enter my mind that it could have been spirits."* Neither Margaret nor Janet could remember which rooms these men slept in, or whether or not it could have been the same room.

The most frequently seen ghost in the Garrison Inn is described as an Abe Lincoln looking character, with top hat, beard, lanky frame and dark colored clothes. *"I've seen him more than once,"* said Chris Gissel the bartender. *"He's usually hanging around in the basement, near the bar area. He's bearded, dark complected, square shouldered, and tall, but I see him in a wink and then he's gone."* Chris also reported that she and other bartenders have seen glasses explode in the tunnel area of the basement where they are sometimes stored, *"I mean rows of them exploding all at once,"* she said.

Brian says that *"at Christmastime, there was a bus tour, called 'Marley's Ghost Tours,' making the rounds of haunted places on the North Shore, and the folks ate a late dinner here at the Garrison Inn. One elderly lady in the group, who was heading for the Ladies Room, began screaming hysterically that she had seen a ghost in the brick passageway. No one had yet explained to the group that the Inn was haunted, nor could she have known how the ghost was described by others who had seen it in the past. 'Describe what you saw,' I asked her once she was calmed down. 'A middle-aged man,' she said, 'in a sitting position right outside the Ladies Room. He wore a stove-pipe hat and had a beard. He looked something like Abe Lincoln she concluded.'"*

New owner of the Inn, Janet Eisenberg, says that she was told that *"three black ghosts haunt the place too,"* which is all very appropriate for an establishment named for America's foremost Abolitionist. Be the ghosts black or white, however, as Brian says, *"The supernatural just seems to flourish here in Newburyport."* Most of this ghostly activity is underground, flowing out, as Brian says, *"from the spokes of a wheel,"* the hub of which is the Frog Pond—a magically picturesque little body of water that hasn't changed since before the White Man came.

The Garrison Inn of Newburyport was recently purchased by the Eisenbergs of Andover, who were unaware of its haunting history - but the ghosts have since received them warmly.

Fort Foster at Kittery Point, Maine, where the Lady In Red is often seen in ghostly form, hovering over the waters of the Piscataqua River.

Bill Ryan, former mayor of Haverhill, sits before the Old York Graveyard in Maine, telling the story of New England's worst Indian massacre in 1692. Forty victims of the massacre are buried in the graveyard, as is Indian squaw Patience Boston who was hanged for murder in the 1700s and whose ghost is said to haunt the graveyard and nearby jail.

IV
York And Kittery Ghosts

My old friend and secretary, Loretta Rainville, spends a lot of time in the summer vacationing with her husband, Roger, in Southern Maine. Some of their leisure time is spent with the Slipkowskys, Barbara and Jack, who own a summer cottage at York Beach. Roger is a history buff and Loretta loves antiques, so the Slipkowskys always plan to tour some local place of historic interest when the Rainvilles come to visit.

On this one beautiful sunny day in July, Loretta remembers, *"We visited an old fort on the Kittery side of the Piscataqua River. The moment we entered the grounds overlooking the water, I felt I had been there before, but I knew I never had been. There will be a pier on the left,"* she told the others, before they reached the water's edge. But there was no pier, only the outcroppings of pilings of what once was a pier.

"The others looked at me strangely and I surely felt strange," said Loretta. *"I wanted to leave, but felt impelled to stay. I then experienced a weather change, which the others with me later stated that they did not experience. The wind picked up and it became foggy. I felt chilled and then experienced a deep sense of sadness. Looking out to where a pier once stood, I saw and felt the presence of a young woman. She stood there, looking mournfully out to sea. She wore a long red dress with calico trim. Her long brown hair was tousled by the wind and her slender white body trembled. I could not clearly see her face, for I was looking at her from the side, but I felt her deep loneliness, and almost felt that I was her. It was an eerie feeling, and I was truly frightened. I told the others that I must leave and they obliged, believing that I had suddenly become ill. It was misty and windy and near dusk to me when we left the site of the old fort, but the others later assured me that the weather hadn't changed.*

It was still a lovely July day when we left the area. The deep sadness of the apparition remained with me for many hours which was in marked contrast to the happy, cheerful mood we were all in when we arrived at the ancient site. To this day, I am still plagued with the questions, who was this woman, and why did I see and experience her loneliness, when none of the others with me did? Was she truly a ghost? Why were her feelings so intense and why were they passed on to me?"

"What would you do if you had a similar experience today?" I asked Loretta.

"I think I would be more comfortable with that feeling today," said Loretta, *"but then I was frightened and confused....I would like to comfort her, whoever she was or is and because only I picked up her presence that day, I feel that*

there must be some kind of communion between us. I am at a loss, however," concluded Loretta, *"as to why I alone experienced this apparition, for I have never experienced anything like it, before or since that day at Kittery, Maine."*

Loretta's encounter occurred on the grounds of Fort Foster at Kittery Point at the mouth of the river across from Portsmouth, New Hampshire. Looking straight out to sea from where the young woman in red appeared to Loretta is a small cluster of islands known as The Isles of Shoals, owned jointly by New Hampshire and Maine. English explorer John Smith named the islands after himself in 1614, but no one ever called them *"Smith Islands,"* and they were settled by fishermen about the time the Pilgrims were digging in at Plymouth. Unlike the pious Pilgrims, the *"Shoalers"* were a rough, tough bunch of fishermen, and throughout the 17th and 18th century were thought to harbor pirates in their rocky abode. John Scribner, New Hampshire historian of the 1700s, writes, *"there is strong ground for suspicion indeed, that the Islanders were generally indulgent and sometimes friendly and serviceable in their intercourse with the numerous pirate ships which visited their harbor."*

Isle historian, Celia Thaxter, who grew up at Kittery and on the Isles in the mid-1800s, is more explicit: *"At the time of the first settlement,"* she writes, *"the islands were infested with pirates."* One of the pirates who came to live on the Isles in 1714 was Sandy Scott, alias Sandy Gordon, first mate to Ed Teach, alias Blackbeard. Blackbeard allowed Scott to command a French brig they had plundered together which he renamed the FLYING SCOT, and he sailed her into Gosport Harbor at the isles of Shoals. Soon after, Sandy Scott married Martha Herring on Appledore Island with all the Isles fishermen in attendance. But the honeymoon was interrupted by a British man-o-war hot on the trail of these notorious pirates. The British were seeking Sandy Scot not only for pirating but for mutiny and murder.

Many years earlier, Captain John Herring, commander of the British ship the PORPOISE, whipped Sandy ruthlessly after catching him in bed with his teenaged daughter, Martha. Months later when Sandy had the opportunity, he took revenge. After he and other members of the crew had mutinied, Sandy, in turn whipped Commander Herring with 72 lashes, beating him to death. Apparently, Martha wasn't too fond of her father either, for she then ran off with Sandy and willingly followed him into his profession of piracy.

Not caring to run any longer, Sandy decided that he wanted to set up housekeeping with Martha at the Isles. So, he sailed out in the FLYING SCOT to meet the British warship in battle. Two well-directed broadsides from the British and the FLYING SCOT sank like a rock, Sandy Scott going down with her. Only two members of the pirate crew survived the sinking. They were picked up by the crew of the warship and hanged at the yardarm before sunset. As for Martha Herring, legend has it that she remained on the Isles for years, moving to Kittery about 1730, a destitute soul, constantly pacing the shore expecting her beloved Sandy Scott to return. She died in despair, supposedly at Kittery, in 1735. Celia Thaxter tells us, *"Teach's comrade, Captain Scott, brought this lovely lady hither...They buried immense treasure on the islands...that of Scott was buried...apart from the rest....The maiden was carried to...where her pirate lover's treasure was hidden, and made to swear with horrible rites, that until his return, if it were not till the day of judgement, she would guard it from search of all mortals. So, there she paces still...She laments like a Banshee before the tempest, wailing through the gores at Appledore."*

Could Loretta Rainville's apparition be that of Martha Herring, one wonders, still waiting some 275 years later for the return of her hot-headed Scotsman? Or is this lonesome spirit at Kittery Point another heart sick young woman, who looks longingly beyond the Isles far out to sea for a lover who will never return? Possibly the Martha Herring legend is coincidental to Loretta's experience. But when one bit more of the tale is told, it does add some credence to Loretta's apparition being Martha.

Sandy, when in battle, always wore a bright red uniform. He was wearing it the day he died. He was wearing it at his wedding on Appledore Island, and to match his bright attire that day, Martha too wore red, *"a stunning red dress that was her wedding gown."* If, as Celia Thaxter writes, *"Martha Herring guards an immense treasure,"* then that treasure must be at Kittery Point, as desolate a spot now as it was then. One might think that, having heard of the Martha Herring legend, Loretta Rainville had hallucinated about the lady in red standing on a disintegrated pier, but Loretta was and probably still is unaware of the legend. She is not one to tell tall tales, nor does she believe in ghosts, yet she assures me that what she saw that day on the grounds of Fort Foster at Kittery Point was real to her and not a hallucination. Her husband, Roger, a severe skeptic of ghosts and hauntings, admits that his wife was *"terrified that day of something she saw hovering over the water."* The Martha Herring Legend only adds to the mystery.

* * * * * * * * * *

In the neighboring town of York, as in Kittery, there are many creaky old houses that lend themselves perfectly to supposed hauntings by unseen spirits. A few of these homes date back to the 1600s and many are of 18th century vintage. Although considered part of New England's wilderness well into the 1700s, the area had been permanently yet sparsely settled since about 1623. In 1690, Indian raiders attacked Kittery, burning the scattered farmhouses and barns one by one, killing 88 men, women and children. In 1692, 400 hostile Indians wearing snowshoes and led by French officers from Canada, attacked York on February

5th, *"Candlemas Day,"* killing or capturing 300 villagers. Every home on the upper side of the river was destroyed. Only the old gaol, built in 1656, the Garrison house, and the Meeting House were still standing when the Indians departed with over 100 captives on a month-long trek through the mountains back to Canada.

Among their captives was four year old Jeremiah Moulton, who amused the Indians with his many escape attempts. Finally the Indians just let him go, and he miraculously made his way back to civilization. In years to come, the Indians regretted their decision, for Moulton, some years later became Sheriff of York County, and was celebrated as a ferocious Indian fighter. His home was the York Jail, one of the buildings left standing after the Massacre of 1692. It was while Moulton was sheriff that timbers from the gaol were used in building a new York jail in 1719. But it was then that the sheriff faced a new Indian menace, an unruly inmate and Abernaki squaw named Patience Boston. When she came to Moulton she was wild, wanton and pregnant to boot. She had murdered a child, son of a local minister who had attempted to tame and Christianize her. Patience drowned his son in a well and also tried to poison him and his wife. She spent almost two years in the jail, but once her own son was born and weaned she was hanged. According to many, however, her spirit lingers on in the old York Gaol which is now a museum.

The Old Gaol museum guides, or *"interpreters"* as they are called, constantly feel the presence of Patience Boston in the jail, especially upstairs where dangerous inmates were once held. *"I feel spooky about four thirty, when I have to start closing up,"* says interpreter Kristan Start, *"and there was an interpreter here before me who refused to go in the jail to close up, for she said she felt a presence that frightened her."*

The present caretaker and groundskeeper at the Old Gaol complex, is Dana Moulton, descendant of former sheriff and Indian fighter Jeremiah Moulton. Although a ghost skeptic, he too feels the presence of disturbed spirits at the jail, especially at night. One night recently, he was driving by the jail and saw that a light was on in the house next door to the jail, the Emerson-Wilcox House, which is part of the museum-complex. He entered the house to shut off the light and was greeted with moans, groans and the sounds of footsteps in the old house. When he approached the lamp that he thought had been mistakenly left on during the day, it went off by itself. Dana left the house in a hurry, and refuses to enter the Emerson-Wilcox House at night. Coincidentally, fronting the jail and the old house, is a graveyard. Interred in it are the victims of the 1692 York Indian massacre, including Dana's ancestors.

Less than half a mile or so up the road from the Old Gaol, is another building that supposedly was standing on the day of the Indian raid. Today it is known as the Brickyard Restaurant, and if circumstantial evidence is enough to declare a

The Old York Gaol, built in 1719, where Patience Boston was an inmate before she was executed. It is still one of her favorite haunts.

Proprietor Bill Johnson stands outside of Orchard Farm Tavern, of York, Maine, now "The Brickyard," where ghosts have pestered him and his employees since he renovated the place in the late 1980s.

place haunted, then York's Brickyard, located near the Kittery border at Route One, is a bonafide haunted house.

In 1990, it was known as the Orchard Farm Tavern, converted from an old farmhouse into a large kitchen, bar, lounge and four small dining rooms. Bill Johnson, a local boy, was the proprietor, with Sean Spellman and Brad Mason, the chefs. Prior to renovations in the late 1980s, the Danforth family lived there. According to a young woman who was married to one of the Danforth boys and wishes to remain anonymous, *"Weird things happened in this house, especially upstairs. Bob Danforth saw the ghost of a little girl, aged about ten, with long, blond hair, standing at the top of the stairs one day, and from that day on, he refused to sleep in his bedroom upstairs."* According to Mrs. Danforth, someone committed suicide in one of the rooms upstairs, and his spirit lingers there still, *"an unhappy, angry spirit."* Bill Johnson said that, *"the elder Mrs. Danforth, when she sold the place, was convinced the place was haunted and had accepted the ghosts as part of the family."*

Prior to the Danforths, the King family and Tom Davidson, who ran a Black Angus Farm and sold homemade ice cream, lived in the house. The barn, once located some 100 yards behind the house on the York River, was also used to store bricks when Orchard Farm was earlier converted into a brickyard. Although Bill Johnson uncovered an old Indian escape hatch in the house during his renovations, Virginia Spiller, librarian of the York Historical Society, doesn't believe the house dates back to the 1600s, but possibly to the mid-1700s and, therefore, may not have been standing during the terrible Indian massacre of 1692. A mortician, so chef Brad Mason informed me, once lived and performed his business in the house, and the residue of his activities may have produced the ghosts that haunt the place.

"Except for an office in the back," says Brad, *"the rest of the place was once a morgue. When I have to come in here alone in the early morning, which is often, I sometimes feel the cold presence of spirits here, especially in the back storage room, It gives me the chills. I also hear banging, heavy pounding on the walls that continues on for some time, which really unnerves me. Also, windows open and close right before my eyes. But the most frightening morning greeting from the ghosts, is when I find all the candles on the tables lit, after I had carefully extinguished them the night before and I closed up for the night. Bill Johnson has been with me when we entered the restaurant in the morning to find all the candles, some eighteen of them, burning away, after we snuffed them out eight hours before and then locked up for the night."*

When I visited Orchard Farm Tavern in 1990, Bill Johnson confirmed Brad's experiences. *"We would put the candles out very carefully every evening,"* said Bill, *"for fear of fire, but when we returned in the morning, the candles were lit. This was very disturbing to me, not only because of the mystery of it, but because of the potential fire hazard. It happened four or five times, and not only did Brad, Sean Spellman and I experience it, but two of the waitresses as well. Emily Caldwell actually saw one candle relight itself one morning, just after she had snuffed out the flame, and when she tried to put it out again, the flame leaped way up high and almost burned her hand. Although everyone who works here got use to the mischievous ghosts, it did give me the jitters, and a waitress and a cook did quit because of these unseen spirits, although they said they were leaving for other reasons....All these weird things began to happen in early 1988, when we began renovations. We had to rebuild the back of the house, and we had to prop up the back wall, but one day the jacks slipped and kicked right out, leaving the wall with no support, but the wall didn't fall. We all ran, expecting a crash, but the wall just remained suspended in air with nothing holding it up. We quickly reset the jacks while invisible hands held up the wall, and it was then that I suspected that the old ghost stories about this place might have some validity.*

I am now convinced, as old Mrs. Danforth was, that this place is loaded with spirits.....I hear them sometimes when I'm upstairs in my office, whispering, crying, or laughing. At first I thought the sounds were coming from the kitchen or dining room, but they're not. They're coming from up here on the second floor, and most of the time, I'm up here alone. I often hear muffled sobs coming from the closet," said Bill Johnson, *"and one of twelve psychics who have visited here within the last few years, told me that a little girl spirit hides in the closet, because another middle-aged male spirit is constantly yelling at her....This psychic had no knowledge of the little girl ghost that others had seen and that I had heard crying, yet she described her as having long blond hair, and as being about ten to eleven years old. When that psychic left here, she was pale as a ghost herself, and was sweating gum-drops. She really seemed to put her heart and soul into her work, and almost all the psychics, who have come here separately, have concluded that a little girl stands near the top of the stairs, supposedly frightened by the ghost of a mean man...I know it all may sound silly, but I'm convinced that something or someone haunts this place."*

The hauntings didn't sound silly to me, and I thought it would be a good place for my diligent ghost-buster, Brian-the-monk, to spend some time. Coincidentally, it was my former secretary, Loretta Rainville, who told me about this haunted tavern of York in the first place, after she had dinner here and was introduced to Bill Johnson. I invited Brian to dinner at Orchard Tavern, and with my friend Bill Ryan, former Mayor of Haverhill, drove up to York one blustery autumn evening. After dinner, Bill Johnson had invited us to stay the night upstairs in the restaurant in what was then his office, so that Brian might collect further information or possibly even get a photograph of one of the ghosts.

Brian arrived at the tavern as enthusiastic as ever, with all his equipment: infra-red camera, binoculars, and a tape recorder. From the moment we sat down to eat, I realized it was probably a mistake to have brought Bill Ryan along. Brian showed Bill all the religious objects he brings with him when confronting ghosts: holy water, rosary beads, and a holy relic of the Catholic Church. Brian is a serious ghost-buster, but the more Brian explained the purposes of the various religious objects necessary when confronting spirits that possibly were evil, the more Ryan seemed to disbelieve Brian's methods, and in fact, ghost hunting in general. He thought the entire process was a waste of time. Bill was too polite to tell Brian that he thought we were chasing rainbows, but when Brian went to the men's room, Bill informed me that he thought both Brian and I had become a bit excessive in our pursuit of ghosts. I assured my friend that I was only looking for good stories, and had no intention of spending the night upstairs waiting to see or hear ghosts. I had rented a room in the motel across the street and intended to get a good night's sleep.

Besides Bill Johnson, three others came to our table that evening to tell us of their experiences working in the tavern and encountering ghosts. Waitresses, Emily and Cindy, assured us that the spirits often set bottles and glasses in the wrong places at the bar to confuse them, and that, from the waitress station, they often heard talking upstairs, when no humans were there.

"Some evenings when I'm here late, stripping the tables after all customers have left, I hear weeping and sobbing of a little girl, coming from the upstairs front room," said Emily. *"I think that was probably her playroom or bedroom when she was a little girl. Maybe she died in that room."*

But who was she, I wondered?

"An artist who used to come here," said Cindy, *"once saw the ghost of the little girl at the head of the stairs, standing on the seventh step, she said, and the little girl was holding something in her right hand, but she couldn't make out what it was."*

A local police officer, Les Bridges, told us that one day he entered the restaurant and asked to make a quick call to headquarters. *"Bill let me use the phone in his upstairs office,"* said Bridges. *"I was in there alone for only a few minutes, when there was a distinct knocking at the office door. I must have said 'Come In!' five times, but the knocks continued. I finally opened the door, but no one was there, and no one else was upstairs. When I closed the door, the knocking continued. When I told Bill about it, he just laughed and said it happens all the time, and it was just the ghost letting me know he was around."*

Bill Johnson said that many had experienced not only the knocking, weeping sounds and whisperings that seem to come from inside his office walls, but that there is a constant slamming of doors upstairs and downstairs, heard many times when no one is in the restaurant but himself.

54

Bill Johnson had clipped an old newspaper article from the June 1st, 1988 issue of the **York Weekly**, framed it and hung it on the tavern wall. *"The Old House on Route One, one of the oldest buildings in York, has been reincarnated,"* it read, *" and if you don't go in much for ghosts, concentrate on the lobster pie."* That's really what I wanted to do that evening, concentrate on lobster pie and other good food which was served up. But both Brian and Ryan were anxious to get upstairs to confront the ghosts, Brian to set up his gear, and Ryan to experience the novelty of being on a ghost-hunt. I knew it wasn't going to work.

Brian was intent on explaining everything to Ryan to convince him that ghost-hunting was valid and that the religious overtones were necessary, but the more Brian went into detail, the more skeptical Ryan became. I also realized that once we were upstairs with tape machine to record sound and infra-red camera to hopefully get a photo, both requiring silence and patience, Ryan would quickly become bored, which he did. He assailed us with little jokes and side-comments, which unnerved Brian, but got me to laughing—not a good mood for ghost hunting. I decided that it would be best to take Ryan away from the ghostly atmosphere so that Brian might get on with the serious side of his mission. Brian brought an audio tape with him which he began playing loudly as Ryan and I left the upstairs for the lounge below. It was *"The Mass For The Dead."* Being a Third Order Franciscan Lay Monk, Brian was performing an exorcism. He held his rosary beads, a wooden cross containing a relic from Saint Catherine, and his infra-red camera. We were leaving him in this classic pose, when I noticed that one of Brian's fingers was missing; his left ring finger.

"When did that happen?" I asked.

"Ten days ago," he replied matter-of-factly, *"An accident in Spain."*

He was completely absorbed in his work. So I headed across the street to the motel. Ryan was hobnobbing with Johnson in the bar. I was tired, only a few months back from the hospital after undergoing open heart surgery, but I felt guilty leaving Brian upstairs alone to bravely face the spirits, which he considered to be dangerously evil. He'd be forced to stay up almost all night, only a few days after losing a finger. I never did ask him how the accident occurred or what he was doing in Spain, but just assumed that monks live strange lives and it was really none of my business.

Picking up the key to my room, I told the motel clerk that another man would be coming over soon and that a third might appear in the middle of the night, and I explained to him about our ghost hunting venture.

"Oh, we have a ghost here too," he said. *"I don't know why, but our Room 233 is haunted...Would you like to stay in it, it's vacant?"*

"No," I replied, having had enough to do with ghosts that evening. *"But, if possible, I'll take the room next to it, just in case my ghost-buster friend has*

extra energy to take on your ghost once he spends the night across the street."

With the key to Room 231, as I passed 233, I put my hand on the doorknob and surprisingly felt that old familiar electrical pulsation in my hand. *"That place is haunted alright,"* I said aloud to a long empty corridor.

When Ryan arrived about an hour later, I had him pass his hand over the outside of the door to Room 233. He too got a tingling sensation through his hand, which became even stronger when he pressed his flesh to the doorknob.

"What causes that?" Ryan asked. I explained as best I could about something I didn't really understand myself.

"It's an evil electricity, according to Brian, a sensation caused by spirits to those who are sensitive to ghosts, and apparently you and I are both catalysts for spooks."

When Brian came to the motel room at about 2:00 a.m., exhausted from an unfruitful vigil, Ryan told him about the room next door, but Ryan had been joking so much earlier in the evening, that Brian didn't take him seriously about the room being haunted. Brian explained to us for about a half hour how he purified the building across the street with his exorcism and how he hoped the people who worked there would not be bothered by ghosts again. I was afraid that if he started exorcising the room next door, I'd get no sleep.

"If you keep trying to get rid of all these ghosts, I'll have nothing to write about," I told him.

Ryan finally told Brian to shut up, and we all got some sleep.

Six months later, Brian visited Orchard Farm Tavern once again to check on the ghosts. Bill Johnson said that except for an incident only a few days after his exorcism the place had been quiet. An old-fashioned iron, used to keep the front door open, flew into the restaurant one morning, the door slamming shut behind it. *"It was like the ghost was leaving the place angry, and flipped the iron into the restaurant as a goodbye gesture,"* said Bill to Brian. It wasn't too long afterwards that Bill Johnson did the same thing, leaving Orchard Farm Tavern for work elsewhere. The new proprietor is Brad Leigh and he changed the name of the restaurant to 'The Brickyard.' Emily Caldwell and Brad Mason stayed on as waitress and cook at The Brickyard, and I called Brad recently to ask if all was quiet as Brian had reported.

"Yes, it's been pretty good lately," Brad admitted, *"but Emily did have a weird experience the other day, near the coffee maker. She was alone, with no one around her, and a hollow, gruff voice came from out of nowhere and said, 'Stop! Don't Do That,'"*

"What did she do?" I asked Brad.

"She ran out of the restaurant," Brad laughed.

"So the ghosts are still active, even after Brian's exorcism?"

"Well, the psychics say there is more than one ghost here. Maybe he got rid

of one or two of them."

Brad's new boss, Brad Leigh, is more skeptical of the presence of ghosts than Bill Johnson was.

"I haven't seen or heard anything," said Brad Leigh, *"but my wife hears those strange knocking sounds and whisperings that Johnson talked about. Jane, one of our waitresses said that three elderly ladies came here to eat the other day and asked her, 'How many people have died in this place?' They were serious, Jane said. They told her that they could feel the presence of many spirits."*

"But nothing else unusual has happened there in the last year?" I asked.

"Well, come to think of it," said the new proprietor, *"there was something quite unusual....A large painting that I hung on the wall came crashing down one day and slid across the dining room as if someone had flung it. It actually bounced a couple of times and landed in the middle of the room. We thought surely it had smashed, but when we picked it up we were surprised to find that the glass hadn't broken. The marvel of it was that the painting was hung on the wall with fingerhooks, quite securely, and the fingerhooks weren't bent or broken. It was as if the painting was lifted off the wall and then dropped. No one was even near it when it fell."*

"Where did the painting come from?" I asked.

"I found it stashed away in an old barn," said Brad.

"What is the painting about..What's the subject?"

"It's called 'The Golden Stairs,' and it's just a picture of stairs. There's nothing spooky about stairs is there?"

"No," I replied, *"unless there's a little girl standing at the top of them."*

"Well, I hate to tell you this," said Brad, *"but that's where this picture was hanging—right at the foot of the stairs where others have seen the ghost."*

"Well, I hate to tell YOU this, Brad," I replied, *"but like it or not, I think that little ghost is still hanging around your Brickyard!"*

Beverly Cove, once owned by Thomas Lothrop, is now peppered with antique homes and mansions, three of which contain ghosts that may date back to Lothrop's time, the early 1600s. Photo by Steve Harwood.

V
The Flower of Essex

There are three houses in an area known as Beverly Cove, facing the Atlantic Ocean and only a few miles from my own home, that I and others who know their history have deemed haunted. I wasn't introduced to these three homes all at once, but piecemeal: a call from a friend about one; my daughter, babysitting, in another; a frightened man asking me to investigate the third—all within a period of three to four years. All three homeowners asked that I keep their identity anonymous and that I don't reveal the exact locations of these haunted houses to anyone. This request is not unusual, for people don't want their privacy disturbed by curious sight-seers, nor do they want friends and relatives to avoid visitations because of frightening spirits that dwell within. It is also now a law in Massachusetts that if a house is haunted, the owner must disclose this information if and when he or she attempts to sell or rent the house. And these three owners didn't want that blight upon their homes, even though the stigma is obviously there.

One of the owners was quite pleased that a ghost shared the dwelling with her and her husband, although the husband wasn't that thrilled about it. Another of the owners was quite upset about sharing his quarters with a ghost and feared for the safety of his family. The third owner denied that the ghost was there, yet friends and guests who visited the house were well aware of its presence. *"Every time I went to the house, I saw it,"* Peter B. said to me. *"It was a white wisp in human form, always seemingly going up the front stairs near the living room. My friend and his wife seemed to ignore it, so I never said anything to them, but they had to see it...I mean, they lived there. It couldn't just happen when my wife and I came to visit. Yet, they never said anything about it, so, to be polite, we never did either. And it wasn't just me who saw it, my wife did too, but she won't talk about it. She thinks she heard somewhere that there once was a murder in the house, so maybe it's the ghost of the murder victim. And we both agree that the apparition was that of a woman."*

Besides the hauntings, one thing that I thought was peculiar is that two of these houses are located not more than 200 yards from each other, and the third is but half a mile away. I wondered if there was any connection between them, any common denominator that would link the three ghosts or the three houses. The haunting spirits are very dissimilar: a seemingly harmless Puritanical ghost of a woman, an angry, almost poltergiestic kind of evil spirit, and a prankish male spirit that likes to frighten babysitters. There seemed to be nothing similar about these ghosts, but after some research at the local library and courthouse, I found information connecting the three houses—they were all built on land once owned by the same man, Thomas Lathrop, sometimes spelled Lothrop. Ghost experts say that humans who become ghosts after death are often those who died tragically or quickly—no one had a more surprising or tragic end in the history of Massachusetts than Thomas Lathrop. His death in 1675 was the talk of America and the woesome pain of all New England, especially in Essex County. He was revered as the commander of *"The Flower Of Essex,"* and he and his men are remembered to this day in Western Massachusetts, as *"The Butchered Of Bloody Brook."*

Captain Lathrop was considered a hero in the County of Essex. He had fought the French and the Indians, commanded an expedition to Acadia, and once commanded the forces at Port Royal, Nova Scotia. He was a member of the General Court and a Deputy of the new town of Beverly, where he had purchased much land from the Indians. Although he and his wife had no children of their own, they took in orphans. And as historian Charles Upham writes, *"The children thus from time to time domesticated in the family, and called him father, and he addressed them as his children."* In 1650, he had gone to England and persuaded his sister Ellen to return with him to America, promising her that when he died he would leave her his estate in Beverly. His wife, Bethia Rea Lathrop, apparently was not aware of this agreement with his sister.

At the outbreak of the Indian War, commonly known as King Philip's War, volunteers were called for to join Captain Lathrop's company to fight the Indians who were ravaging Western Massachusetts. Over eighty young men, most of them teenagers from Beverly, Cape Ann, and surrounding towns, joined Lathrop in the march west. They all hailed from Essex County, and were so enthusiastic and full of vitality, that they were dubbed, *"The Flower of Essex."*

"Our soldiers never meet with any savages," one boy wrote home disappointedly eight weeks after marching off with Lathrop *"we only drive them further westward, where they gathered all the Indians they could at their party about Pecomptuck."* Pecomptuck, known today as Deerfield, was where King Philip, on September 14, 1675, forced all settlers to abandon their homes and to leave behind some 300 bushels of wheat that was being preserved in the fields. Four days later, Lathrop and his boys were sent to Deerfield with eighteen teamsters and their wagons to gather this wheat and bring it to the western military outpost at Hadley. It was a hot day, and having successfully gathered the wheat and traveled more than half way to Hadley, Lathrop allowed his men to rest at Muddy Brook in South Deerfield, drink from the flowing waters, bathe in it if they wished, and eat all the ripe grapes that grew wild on vines at the edge of the forest. Most of the soldiers, unfortunately, left their muskets in the wagons as they walked deeper into the woods to find and munch on the succulent grapes. They were suddenly attacked by over 700 Indians, ambushed from every direction without warning. It was over within minutes.

Lathrop, his company of teenagers and the teamsters were wiped out with but seven survivors. One was 18 year old John Toppan of Newbury. After being hit with two arrows, he fell, *"and I covered myself with weeds so that the Indians couldn't see me, and sometimes they stepped right over me."* Another survivor of the massacre was Henry Bodwell of Ipswich, who, with a musketball lodged in his left arm, battled the oncoming Indians *"by swinging my musket, and I made it through the line of them and escaped."* Robert Dutch of Ipswich was miraculously spared after being shot in the head and half scalped. The Indian who was cutting his head off, left him to kill someone else, and he lived. The three survivors reported that Captain Lathrop himself was one of the first to be killed.

Captain Lathrop left no will, and the dispute over the land he owned, where the three haunted houses are located, lasted for years. His sister Ellen, married to schoolmaster Ezekiel Cheever of Ipswich, and the mother of many children, claimed her brother's property. The Captain's widow Berthia, of course, wanted the land, but if it couldn't go to her she felt it should go to her adopted children and to her brother Joshua Rea's children. To complicate matters, the widow remarried only eight months after the Bloody Brook Massacre. Lawsuits were filed, but even six years later, an order from the General Court read: *"The antiquarians have been sorely perplexed in the determining of the relationship of the Cheevers and Reas, as they appear to be connected together as heirs of the Lathrop property."*

Finally, the Captain's widow relented and agreed to surrender all claims if the Cheevers would pay her sixty pounds sterling, which they did by selling a home in Salem to one Nicholas Noise, one of the villainous ministers of the 1692 witch hysteria. But those were the disturbances then, what of the disturbances on this land today? Is there any connection with these ancient disputes, the bloody massacre, and the ghosts that haunt the houses on this land today?

Al Janard, John Silva and Phil Renard, three local carpenters, were given a job to renovate some upstairs rooms in one of the old houses in Beverly. The house was built in 1671, and owned by Thomas Whittredge, who had served with Lathrop in the Port Royal Expedition. It had been part of the Lathrop estate. The owner, Barbara Purcell, (not her real name) is a superb gardner, interior decorator, and antique collector. She and her husband Bill bought the house some twenty years ago, because the house itself is an antique and has extensive lush gardens and an orchard out back. She furnished the downstairs in period furniture, some being replicas for 17th century furniture. Her plans were now to enlarge some of the little rooms on the second floor and carve herself out a half decent sized bedroom and a modern bathroom. After all, this 17th century living can go just so far. The carpenters understood what she wanted. But before they began their work she called them into her large kitchen with the walk-in fireplace, sat them down with coffee and muffins at the kitchen table, and in all seriousness, warned them that the house was haunted.

"From the day I moved in," she told them, *"the neighborhood kids told me that this place was haunted, and I told them that was just fine with me. The ghost very shortly made herself known to me. They said that her name is Elizabeth, and she is a Puritan woman, very refined and sweet. Certainly no one to be afraid of."*

Phil looked at Al and smiled. He expected Mrs. Purcell to smile too at any moment and say it was all a joke, but she didn't.

"I'm serious boys, and I'm sure you're going to meet up with her before your work is completed here, so I'm giving you fair notice. She loves to play little games with people, so be prepared."

Phil shook his head in disbelief, but Al said, *"I believe you."* He couldn't help smiling, however, and Mrs. Purcell shook her finger at him.

"You'll be sorry if you don't," she told him.

"I really do believe," said Al, *"I really do."*

The first day or two on the job went without incident. *"We hardly ever went onto the first floor,"* said Al, *"and only now and then did any of us have to go into the basement, usually to shut off the electricity, but most of the time we were on the second floor or in the attic, which was full of spiderwebs. On the third day, when Mrs. Purcell was out of the house, Phil had to go out to the truck for some special tool he needed, but he wasn't gone two seconds, when he came running back up the stairs yelling to John and me. He sure looked scared. His eyes were bulging out. He was all out of breath when he told us that the old rocking chair in the living room at the foot of the stairs, was rocking back and forth. I laughed, but John didn't. Phil got mad at me, took me by the arm and led me down the stairs. There was a black cat sitting on the bottom stair staring into the living room. It, too, had its eye on the rocking chair that was rolling back and forth on the wide floorboards as it someone was sitting in it. Phil's face was white and looked at me in disbelief. The rocking chair, however, didn't frighten me at all. The cat was probably sitting in the chair and jumped off when she heard you coming, I explained to Phil."*

"Couldn't be," said Phil, *"cause the cat was here on the stairs when I came down the first time, and anyway, the chair would have slowed down by now if the cat had done it, but look at it, it's still going strong. I went over and stopped the chair,"* said Al, *"but it did kind of give me the willies. John was so frightened that he wouldn't even come down and look, but he didn't want to stay alone upstairs either. Phil, after that incident, was as jumpy as a tadpole. He saw the Puritan lady in every dark corner of the attic, and when the cat came around us, he was even more jittery. The cat made me kind of nervous too*

though, 'cause it always looked like it was scared of somethin'. It would stare into dark rooms and meow, or it would jump out at Phil or John from some alcove and make them shout some obscenity at it.

Then there was the morning that Phil had to go into the cellar to shut off the electricity. The cellar door, which was in the kitchen, had a latch lock on it. It was just about impossible that it could lock by itself, but it did, trapping Phil in the damp, dark cellar. He, at first thought John and I had locked him in. He pounded and screamed, but we were in the attic and it was almost an hour before we realized he was missing. We were up there happily pounding away, when John said he thought he heard Phil's voice. By the time I got down there to unlock and open the door, Phil's voice was as hoarse as a haddock, and his fists were red raw from pounding. Most of all though, he was scared silly. He said that at first he thought it was us who done it, but then he knew it was the ghost. Phil just wasn't the same on that job since that morning. Phil had a heart problem anyway, and he was poppin' nitroglycerine pills on a regular basis until the job was done, which was about three weeks later. I never felt too good in there after that either. I always felt that someone or some thing was looking over my shoulder while I was working, and doors were forever slamming and opening by themselves in the house, especially it seemed when we knew that Mrs. P. wasn't at home. On our last day, our work complete, Phil and I went into the kitchen, made coffee, lifted our cups and shouted in unison, 'Bye bye Elizabeth,' and there came a tremendous loud crash from the living room. We rushed in to see what had fallen, but everything was in order—except the rocking chair was rocking full tilt, and Phil had just let the cat out the backdoor. Phil let out a moan, grabbed his tools in the kitchen and walked out of that house, never to return again, and I was close behind him."

When Phil and Al told me their story I decided to talk to Barbara and Bill Purcell about their resident ghost, and asked that Brian-the-monk be allowed to take infra-red photos in the house. They agreed. From the moment I entered the old house I had that strange numbing feeling, almost nausea, that I seem to feel when ghosts are around. Brian got it too. He calls it *"motion sickness."* He explained to Barbara and Bill that the infra-red film in his camera is sensitive to heat energy and will record any energetic spirits on the film that happen to get in the way of his constantly clicking lens. Barbara gave him the run of the house. So, with rosary beads clutched in one fist and the camera in the other, Brian left the kitchen for the upper floors, saying to Elizabeth the Puritanical ghost as he left us, *"I hope, dear lady that you're nice enough to let me take your picture."* Strangely, when Brian left the room, my pins-and-needles sicky feeling left me, and I thought to myself, maybe the ghost went off with him. Later I discovered that I might not have been wrong in my presumption.

63

Barbara, a beautiful, middle-aged interior decorator, explained to me that she had wanted to live in this house for years before it came up for sale, and she had her husband buy it without ever seeing the inside of it. It was months before she could move in, for much of the interior was in disrepair and Bill did most of the initial renovations. Bill doesn't believe in ghosts, but admits that a lot of strange things do happen in the house. *"When I first started working in here, there was a ringing sound. At first I thought it was a neighbor's phone, but it was coming from inside the house, upstairs somewhere. I searched and searched for the sound but never found it. After awhile I just paid no more attention to it and it went away in about six months."*

"Then there was the time the ghost stole your favorite brown shirt," Barbara reminded him.

He nodded. *"I had placed it carefully on a hanger in the closet and next morning it was gone. We found it months later stuffed into a shoebox on the other side of the house. It took my college class ring too,"* Bill recalled. *"Put it on the fireplace mantel in the kitchen for only a few minutes, returned from a chore, and it was gone. And it's still missing. There's no explanation for it. No one could have taken it, it couldn't have fallen. It just disappeared."*

"She loves to snitch stuff," said Barbara matter-of-factly. *"She apparently loves, or did love, to knit too. I lost five needles while I was knitting one sweater, and lost over twenty needles since I've been here. Like Bill's ring, these weren't misplaced needles, they were snatched up by her. I would drop one by the chair, or put them in the chair seat to leave for a moment, and when I returned, they were gone. One day she took my irreplaceable blue cable needle. I walked to the middle of the room and shouted into the ceiling: 'Okay lady , you've got my needle. I've had it with you, now give me that cable needle back.' It took her awhile, but a few days later I heard this clicking sound from the kitchen stove, and sure enough, I walk into the kitchen and there's the blue needle sitting on the floor in front of the stove. The same thing happened one day when I found my special ball of yarn missing. I shouted aloud for the yarn in an angry voice. When I got up next morning, my bedroom closet door was open, and there was the ball of yarn, rolled out from the closet door to my bed."*

"She took my sports jacket too," piped in Bill, *"but I never got that back. But then I never demanded it back either."*

"I think spirits are attracted to me," said Barbara, *"a spiritualist told me that once, and I'm sure our Elizabeth likes me. Even when Bill's out, I never feel alone in the house with her here."*

"How do you know her name's Elizabeth?" I asked.

"It might not be," Barbara replied. *"It may be Gertrude. I was told that an old spinster named Gertrude lived here in the late 1800s, and she loved to knit, so maybe she's the one stealing all the needles."*

"We were also told by Sam Sayward or Art Thompson, two old historians of

the area, that two children froze to death before this grand old fireplace, sometime in the 1800s."

"Makes you wonder who was the culprit responsible for keeping that fire going, doesn't it," added Barbara. *"It was Sam Sayward who told us when we first moved in here, 'Wait til you see the old woman rocking by the fireplace,' and it was he who said that her name was Elizabeth. He came over here one day and laughingly said to me, 'I hope you realize that you bought a haunted house', but I told him I kind of liked the idea, and I do. I put our rocking chair right by the fire, and as Al and Phil told you, she often rocks away, sometimes late into the night."*

"That's right," confirmed Bill, *"you can hear the chair rocking at night, and I've seen it rock by itself."*

"Can't it be the cat jumping off the seat that causes the rocking?" I asked.

Barbara shook her head *"No".*

"Could be," drawled Bill, *"cept the cat sleeps with us up in the bed, and I've heard the chair rocking, with the cat purrin' in bed beside me. Might be wind from the chimney though,"* suggested Bill. *"The damper is usually up in the winter, however, unless there's a fire going, but in the summer, little birds called chimney swifts dart up and down the chimney into the fireplace. They dart up and down with the wind currents and look like little flying cigars, so there must be enough breeze to push a rocking chair."*

"Except for the fact that it rocks in the winter too, when the damper is closed, blocking out the wind. I'm afraid gentlemen," smiled Barbara, *"that you've just got to face the facts, and that is that we have a sweet, contented old lady ghost living with us. There are, however, days when she can be cantankerous, like the day she stole my car keys. I know that many people lose or mislay their car keys, but I know that I put them on the kitchen counter. When I was ready to go, they were gone. I looked everywhere. I called mother, friends, I screamed, I fretted. I couldn't go anywhere all day. When I finally gave up, after shouting twice at the ghost 'Give me my keys,' I heard a 'clink', and there they were, back on the kitchen counter. Also, one day, while leaving the house, I climbed into my car and noticed that the front light over the outer door was on. I went back inside and shut it off. When I returned to the car it was on again. This ritual continued twice, until I went back in and unscrewed the lightbulb. When I returned home from my errand, the lightswitch was in the 'on' position. Apparently, Elizabeth doesn't know how to screw in lightbulbs."*

Bill went off to an evening meeting and Barbara gave me a tour of the upstairs of the house. In some rooms I had to duck my head, the ceilings were so low and the floors squeaked as we walked around, typical of old homes, but unnerving to nervous types who might think the sounds are caused by ghosts. As we toured the grand old house, Barbara surprised me by revealing that someone had seen the ghost of Elizabeth, but she wasn't seen in this house.

"When I go on vacation to Florida in the winter," said Barbara, *"I invite Elizabeth to pack up her goodies and to come with us to Cape Coral, Florida for a couple of weeks. She obviously does just that, for last year the Currans of Salem joined us and one night their daughter Lacy, a teenager, was sitting at the kitchen table and let out a blood-curdling scream. We all rushed into the kitchen, and Lacy was shivering uncontrollably. She had seen a ghost in the doorway, she told us. 'It was a woman in a big white collar, wearing, what Lacy called, 'a long prairie dress,' similar looking to an old Puritan dress. Lacy said 'her head, in a white bonnet, was touching the top of the doorway, and her feet were floating off the floor.' The poor kid was terrified and I had no doubt that the ghost she saw was Elizabeth, who had decided to join us on vacation."*

As Barbara and I ventured from room to room, she, obviously pleased at showing me her antiques, a voice stopped us before entering one dark room. *"Hold it, don't enter, I'm changing film."* It was Brian. I had almost forgotten about him. He was hiding in a small bedroom. He told us through the door that he had taken 72 photos. When he finished changing his film in the dark, he snapped on the light and we were allowed to enter.

Coming into this little room, with weird, palmtree murals for wallpaper, I got that old pins-and-needles feeling in my face, hands, neck and back. *"I think the ghost is in this room,"* I told Brian. *"She may be just following you around from room to room."*

"I hope so," said Brian.

"This is a spare bedroom," said Barbara, *"and it may be where she sleeps."*

"Saturate this room; it's small enough. Take shots of every inch of it if you can," I said, and so he did.

When the pictures were developed, to my surprise, there was Elizabeth, in her Puritan attire, layed out on the bed in this little room. I couldn't believe my eyes. Brian, however, wasn't pleased with the photo. It was too blurry, he thought. I consider this one of the most amazing infra-red shots he has ever taken, especially knowing that I was in the room when he took it. I had said to him, tongue-in-cheek, *"take the bed, there's a slight indentation on the bedcover, so maybe you've tired her out with all this activity and she's just lying down for awhile"* —And apparently, that's just what Elizabeth was doing, either hamming it up for the camera, or taking a nap.

"I've never met such an obliging ghost," said Brian, *"I guess Barbara's right, She's just real nice to have around."*

Although the ghost's name, Elizabeth, is seemingly lost to antiquity, it's the name all who have lived in the house have always called her, I wonder if the name has not been formalized for "Bethia", the name of Captain Lathrop's wife?

Infra-red photo by Brian-the-monk, shows Puritan woman ghost lying across the bed in the guest room of a 17th century house in Beverly Cove.

One of the three haunted houses of Beverly, built in 1671 by one of Captain Lothrop's soldiers, four years before the butchery of "Bloody Brook."

This was his land, and this house was built here four years before his brutal and sudden death. Could this be where Bethia waited in vain for Captain Lathrop to return from the war?

* * * * * * * * * *

Or, could it be, I wondered, another old house near the cemetery, less than half a mile from the haunted Purcell home? Here lives Fred Kitty, his wife and three children. Fred is a young man, a chef at a local restaurant and seemingly a content man, except for what he calls, *"evil spirits,"* infiltrating his home. He and his wife bought the old house prior to the birth of their third child, and it was shortly thereafter that their second child became extremely ill, and has still not fully recovered. When I told Brian-the-monk of these *"evil spirits"* he gathered up his holy armor of rosary beads, bible, holy water vial and crucifix, and we headed for the home of Fred Kitty (not his real name). With us was Dave Sacconek a professional video man, who Brian invited to take infra-red movies of the house and the backyard, where Fred Kitty said *"these spirits danced some evenings, lit up like little blobs of light and humming a barely discernible chant—like a pack of Indians doing a war dance."*

Describing the spirits as Indians was enough to peak my interest, for while treading Lathrop land, the massacre at Bloody Brook was always paramount on my mind. Before entering the house, Brian said a prayer and spread holy water on the front lawn. I'm not an overly religious man, but realized that even if the ritual didn't help in combating evil spirits, it certainly couldn't hurt.

Fred, his wife and children, and two young babysitters who had haunting stories to tell us, had gathered in the living room. Mrs. Kitty was not happy at having two men roam through her house taking photos and movies of supposed invisible creatures living in their midst. She was noticeably nervous and agitated, but Fred insisted that we continue with our business—me to gather information, while Brian and Dave tried to capture the ghosts on film.

The Kittys and the babysitters informed me that, as with the Purcells, when they first moved into the house there was constant ringing. The Kittys, however, knew where the ringing was coming from—some six phones that were located throughout the house on two floors. Most of the phones were extensions, but often only the extensions would ring and only on the phones that were furthest from anyone in the house. *"By the time I raced to the phone,"* one babysitter told me, *"no one answered."*

But this wasn't just once in awhile, this was continuous, night after night, and nobody was on the line when they answered the phone. This went on, not just for weeks and months but for years, *"and although somewhat subdued as of late, it continues,"* said Fred, *"day and night."* Their sick child also cries day

68

and night and seems to get no comfort, and the combination of noises is unnerving. *"There are other noises too,"* Fred informed me, *"the sounds of a man walking in the attic."*

The babysitters confirmed this as well. *"It's as if someone is up there, constantly walking around in circles."*

Fred also told me that *"part of the attic cannot be accounted for—there's about four-feet of attic in the center of the house that is blocked off, without access to it from either side. There is just no entry to this space, and it's from here that the walking sounds are heard, usually late at night, but I've heard them in the daytime too."* Brian and Dave concentrated on the attic with their infra-red film, and although once developed they got many white blobs, *"Anomalies"* as Brian calls them, they didn't get photos of ghosts in the attic.

Fred took me out into his yard and showed me a 300 pound tree he had recently planted, surrounded by many saplings that were also new additions to his garden. The tree had four heavy wires attached to it, anchoring it in place.

"Why all the wires?" I asked. *"Does the tree fly away if it's not tied down?"*

"Precisely!" Fred replied. *"I brought that tree here in my pickup, and it took two of us to roll it off the truck. It was impossible to lift, the bulb on it had to be some five feet 'round. I planted it without tying it down, and next morning this tree was fifty yards away sitting in the middle of the street with cars trying to maneuver around it. It would take at least five guys to lift that thing with difficulty, and what made it even more remarkable, there was no trail of dirt either in the yard or on the street. It was as if the tree got plucked out of its hole like a flower by some powerful force and then just dropped in the middle of the street."*

Could it be that the enchanting little blue blobs of light that dance and wiggle and skip through Fred's yard periodically at night removed his tree just as a prank? Or was it real husky vandals from the neighborhood—the same ones who occasionally visit the nearby cemetery and tip gravestones over just for the fun of it? We would probably never know.

Fred was perplexed, and we were really no help to him at all. Brian believed that the house was possessed. He sent his photos and Dave's video with the white blobs on them to Malachi Martin, the noted philosopher—priest in New York, author of the book "Hostage To The Devil." Malachi, well versed in such things, agreed with Brian. He, like Brian, apparently, believed that the phenomenon in the house, whatever it might be, was evil.

"It is growing in intensity," Brian concluded, *"and is effecting all who live in that house."* Brian suggested an exorcism, but Fred didn't think the spirits were necessarily evil, so we left the house without a solution to their dilemma. The Kittys, however, separated a few months later.

* * * * * * * * * *

Directly down the street some 200 yards away is another old home, bigger than the Kitty's home and possibly considered a mansion. It has many rambling rooms on three stories, overlooking the sea. Jim and Clara Smart moved into it a few years ago with one child, and they have since had another. My daughter, Keri, became their tenant shortly after they moved in, and she babysat the children to help with her tuition at Gordon College. Her room was on the third floor, but the bedrooms for the Smart family were all on the second floor.

"I always felt uncomfortable sleeping in that room, right across from the door to the attic," Keri told me, *"and one night, coming home late, I tiptoed up the stairs, and as I was entering my room, I heard the attic door squeak open and saw the doorknob turn. I had just moved in, and I was terrified, but I just ran into my room and hid under the covers. I wanted to run downstairs screaming to Clara and Jim, but I didn't want them to think I was a nut. I hardly slept a wink that night. On many a night after that, I'd wake up with a start and hear footsteps in the room below me. It sounded like someone was just walking around the room in circles, and one night the footsteps left the room below me and came slowly up the stairs to my room. I thought it was Clara and I called her name. There was no response. It was like someone was standing outside my room all night and it almost drove me insane."*

When a second child was born to Jim and Clara, it slept in the room below where my daughter heard the footsteps. *"The second child seemed to slow down the restless spirit for awhile. But one night as I stayed up late studying for exams,"* reported my daughter, *"I heard the crackling and rustling of papers coming from my bookcase. I at first thought it was a mouse, and from the corner of my eye I could see some rolled up pieces of paper I discarded earlier begin to move on top of the bookcase. I started to get very frightened, but my fear immediately turned to anger. This old ghost had frightened me just one too many times, I thought. I shouted out loud, 'Whoever you are, I want you to stop this now! I just can't handle this!' My voice was still echoing in the room, when a pile of schoolbooks on my desk, came off the desk, and hit the floor with a thud. I went flying out of the room and quickly down the stairs, bursting into Jim and Clara's room and screaming my head off. I could hold back no longer. 'This place is haunted' I screamed, 'and the ghost is in my room.' Clara calmed me down and then Jim said to her, 'I thought Peter had left.'*

'Who's Peter?' I asked.

'Why our ghost,' he replied. 'He hasn't been active for a long time.'

'Well, he's active now!' I replied.

'Why didn't you tell us he's been bothering you?' Clara asked.

'Cause I thought you'd think I was crazy!' I replied.

'Nonsense,' said Jim, 'he physically pushed me out of the house on the day

70

we moved in here. I had entered the front door of the house and had actually closed the door behind me when this force picked me up and pushed me onto the driveway. He obviously didn't want me living in his house,'

'And from that day on,' Clara said, 'the old servants bells kept ringing day and night, 'til it drove us both out of our wits, so we had to disconnect them, and then the motion alarm detector kept going off as if something was constantly moving through the house. So we changed that system. And then water started pouring into the kitchen from the ceiling and the walls while I was cooking. We had plumbers check it out, and they couldn't find where all the water was coming from. They, in fact, said it was impossible for water to flow into the kitchen like that through the ceiling and walls...I finally just did what you did, I shouted to the ghost 'Cut it out, behave yourself Peter!' I shouted, and he was quiet after that, 'til you came.

I couldn't understand how Jim and Clara knew that the ghost's name was Peter. Were they just guessing I asked? Jim looked at Clara and rolled his eyes into his head. Clara laughed and said, 'yes, at first we were just guessing'. They had made up the name, but one day I was taking a tour in Salem at the Gardner-Pingree House, and the tour guide and I started talking about old houses. When I told her where I lived, she was surprised. Her nephew, she told me, lived in our house, and his name was Peter Cheevers. He had been a real hellion, the woman said, a prankster, and he died fairly young of some disease. She couldn't remember what it was, but he died in the room below where I was sleeping then. That's where I hear the footsteps, I told her. So, Peter is still active in the old house, Dad, if you want to track down another ghost," concluded Keri.

Yes, this one, like the others living nearby on old Lothrop land, intrigued me, for like the others, there was a thread linking this ghost to the ancient conflict of Captain Lathrop and his family. The ghost's name, Clara had discovered, was Peter Cheever, the same surname as the Captain's sister's married name. As the General Court order read in 1681, *"the antiquarians have been sorely perplexed in the determining of the relationship of the Cheevers and Reas, as they appear to be connected together as heirs to the Lothrop property"* —connected together it seems, for over 300 years.

So the conflicts we create in life, may well carry over into after life. The evidence that these ghosts of Beverly Cove are connected with Captain Lathrop in more ways than just his land, is seemingly more than circumstantial, and possibly worthy of further investigation. It is also apparent that the ringing of bells is another spooky incidental that all three haunted places have in common. The Massacre at Bloody Brook, *"The Flower of Essex,"* and Commander Thomas Lathrop may be forgotten in today's fast-paced world, but it seems a spiritual connection lingers on in three old houses at Beverly Cove.

The John Stone Inn, Ashland Massachusetts. (Left), Dana Seaman, part owner of the inn, relates the history of hauntings to the author. It is in this second floor office that the cries and giggles from a little girl ghost are often heard. (Right), Dennis Provencal, Manager of the Inn, tours Bob and Brian through the basement where the ghost of John Stone has been seen and heard. *Inn photo by Butch Adams.*

VI
John Stone's Body Lies A'Moanin

I met the noted parapsychologist ghost-hunter, Raffaele Bibbo when we appeared together on a Boston television show around Halloween time. He had some fascinating stories about his constant pursuit of mysterious spirits, but when I asked him what was the most haunted place he had ever visited, he answered without forethought, *"the John Stone Inn."* It was there, then, that I would bring Brian-the-monk in an attempt to get a photo of whatever it is that haunts the inn. Brian was most acceptable, so we headed out one cool autumn evening in 1991 to hunt ghosts at John Stone's Inn. I, of course, wanted the facts, only the facts. I wasn't going to get spooked. That was not my desire, and Brian only wanted to get a photo of John Stone, the 19th century owner of the inn, who now supposedly haunts the place. We were in Brian's drafty little car, heading for Ashland, but neither one of us knew where Ashland was and had only a vague idea of how to get there.

After pulling off Route 128 and onto the Massachusetts Turnpike, it was only some 10 minutes before we saw the sign for Ashland—a lot closer to home than I had thought, but still, a village seemingly in the middle of nowhere. The inn was downtown, and my second surprise was how close it was to the railroad tracks. As we parked the car behind the inn, we heard the tinkle of a bell and a train came roaring through, the wind from it shaking Brian's little car. Ashland is no bustling metropolis, but I was surprised that only the bell, a couple of blinking red lights, and two automatic crossing gates separated the speeding Amtrack from vehicle and pedestrian traffic on Main Street.

Loaded down with Brian's camera, tape recorder, binoculars, holy objects and infra-red gear, we entered the gloomy old inn, which inside was cheery, bright and filled with loud, jovial people. There were only a few diners finishing up their evening meals in the two downstairs dining rooms, but the bar and lounge were filled with revelers. We were met in the front hall by Dana Seaman, part owner of the inn, and Dennis Provencal, the new general manager, who had worked and lived in the inn in the late 1970s and early 1980s. Dana took us up the long front staircase to his office on the second floor. Dan's brother-in-law, Leonard *"Cappy"* Fournier bought the inn back in 1975, and it was when he began reconstruction of the old building that *"all the strange stuff started happening,"* said Dana. He and the carpenters would lock up the place securely at night, and when they came back in the morning they'd find the place wide open—doors and windows unlocked, some open to the elements. Faucets would turn on by themselves, spurting water all over the place, and upstairs doors were constantly slamming. *"Then we found hidden deep in the dirt cellar, a walled in room with a bunk in it, piled with tattered blankets and an old water barrel. We figured it was a secret room of the underground railroad days used to hide runaway slaves from the South, and speed them off when possible by train to Canada where they could find real freedom,"* said Dana.

"Maybe someone died in that room, and that's where the ghost originated," suggested Brian.

"There's no record of anyone dying here," said Dana, *"not even old John Stone, as far as we know. That is, except for our general manager, John DuBois, but he died in 1984, well after the hauntings began."*

"How did DuBois die?" I asked.

"He was hit by a train, just outside the door, one snowy evening," replied Dana.

I wasn't surprised.

"He and three others were helping a customer push his car off the tracks, March 31st in the midst of a raging blizzard. The others heard the warning bell but apparently he didn't. A west bound Amtrak going fifty miles an hour plowed into him. He either didn't see it coming or he slipped in the snow, but whichever, that was the end of John DuBois. He was only thirty-four years old and really loved by all the workers and steady customers here."

"Word is John saw the ghost of John Stone in the basement only a few nights before he was hit by the train," piped in Dennis, *"and I know that two other managers, Robin Hicks and Butch Adams, have had ghostly encounters right up here in this office, but in both cases, it wasn't the ghost of John Stone, it was a little girl."*

Brian looked at me and rolled his eyes into his head. He was thinking what I was thinking—this sounds like the hauntings at The Brickyard in York, Maine. A little girl and a man haunting the second floor of a tavern. Only coincidence obviously, but children ghosts for some reason seemed sad, and at the same time much more frightening than adult ghosts to me.

"Butch and his girl friend used to be up here on Monday nights when the inn was closed, supposedly to do the books. At about 9:30 p.m., they heard what sounded like a rubber ball bouncing in the corridor, along with the taunting voice of a little girl at play. In a sing-song way, she kept repeating 'la la, la la la.' Butch jumped from his chair and ran into the corridor, but nothing was in the corridor. When he returned to the desk in the office here, the chanting and ball bouncing began again. His girl friend, who is now his wife, insisted that they leave the building. But he stubbornly refused to leave until he had checked out the entire inn. They were both shaking when they left, but Butch was satisfied that no other human being was in the place and that everything was locked up securely. When they returned to the inn next morning, a town policeman stopped Butch on the street and asked if he had a problem at the inn the night before. The policeman said that about midnight, all the lights at the inn on all three floors were blazing brightly, and that he saw Butch's daughter staring out the

window. Butch, of course, didn't have a daughter, and he could only conclude that it was the little girl he had heard playing and singing earlier in the evening."

"It's a little girl ghost about nine or ten years old, and she's been seen or heard by a variety of people, just one of about seven ghosts we have here," smiled Dana Seaman, *"or so the many psychics that hold seances here have told us."*

"We've lost a number of waitresses and bartenders because of her," added Dennis, *"and she's not just here on the second floor. Butch Adams, who worked here some sixteen years, heard her a few times, crying, while he tallied his day receipts in the bar area on the first floor. He also heard her occasionally crying upstairs. Even when six guys were living up here on the second floor in the early 1970s we all heard her, often real late at night, whimpering and crying. Of course, we also heard the typical ghostly knockings and door slammings and the showers would often turn on by themselves, but we all took it in stride."*

Other bartenders and waitresses I interviewed later on in the evening, confirmed the seeing and hearing of the little girl ghost from the cellar to the attic. Bartender Pat Kittredge said, *"I've personally heard laughter from a little child coming from the basement."*

And Peggy Bache, a waitress, reported that, *"More than once, have I heard a ghostly laugh of a little girl, coming from the basement. It gives me chills."*

Waitress Judy Jackson said that her friend Pat Ross lit all the candles on the tables in the large dining room upstairs and they all went out at once, with a whishing sound; and a few months earlier, she had put all the candles out one evening after the dinner guests had left, and they suddenly all were lit again.

"It was enough to almost drive us mad. But even more haunting to my mind," said Judy, *"is the little girl ghost, constantly seen in the little alcove in the kitchen, looking out the window toward the railroad tracks. The people living in the house on the other side of the tracks report to us that they see her often, just staring out, as if in a daze. One of our chefs reported seeing her by the kitchen window several times when he came in first thing in the morning. A little girl with a sweet innocent face and curly brown hair, she would turn to him, smile, and then disappear. It blew his mind. One morning, Cappy the owner and he came in to find that alcove window in the kitchen broken, but it was strangely shattered from the inside and not the outside.."*

Peggy Bache also reported that the former manager of the inn, Robin Hicks, had, like Butch Adams, heard the little girl singing and bouncing her ball up and down the second floor corridor, *"and a few customers have seen her standing in the door of the downstairs dining room, looking out towards the railroad tracks,"* she added.

Raffaele Bibbo, who held a seance at the inn in 1984, and again in 1987 with

75

six different mediums concluded that the little girl was seriously injured at the inn, sometime in the mid-1800s. She had been cared for by one of the Stone brothers, and her mother was a cook in the Inn. This was information gathered by one of the psychics. After much research and interviews with members of the Ashland Historical Society and other historians of the area, I could find no evidence of this girl's existence, nor of any serious accidents at the inn concerning children. But that doesn't mean that the psychic wasn't right. In fact, her conclusion seems quite plausible. Probably the window shattered, maybe just as a train passed and the girl was at her favorite spot at the window. She could have suffered severe lacerations and died and now continues her vigil at the window as a ghost.

Owner Cappy Fournier, once a disbeliever in ghosts, agrees that a train rumbling by could shatter a window and has on occasion shattered glasses and dishes. This may have been an even greater problem during steam engine days, although in those days the trains would usually stop at the inn. Cappy says that his most frightening experience at the inn was when the entire building began shaking violently one afternoon and continued to do so for almost four minutes.

"Was it a freight train?" I asked.

"There was no train going by at the time," he replied, *"and no other building in town shook, so it wasn't an earthquake either."*

John Stone was a wealthy landowner in 1832 when he built the "Railroad Boarding House," now the "John Stone's Inn," at Unionville, now Ashland. He had been discreetly alerted by Boston politicians of the coming of the Boston-Albany Railroad. He built his inn right across the main road from the railroad station. But, I think, even he must have realized after the first train came through that the building was too close to the tracks. In the 1880s, a freight car got loose "up the grade," as they said in the old days, and came barrelling down the tracks, barely missing the inn but smashing into the railroad station and demolishing it. Stone's Inn is made of Ashland brick, which crumbles unless it's painted and is made even more vulnerable by the constant shaking from the trains as they pass. But the inn has endured physically as well as spiritually.

Over 200 people were at the grand opening of the inn, with a military band playing from the roof of a railway coach, and Massachusetts Governor Levi Lincoln giving the main address. Rumor has it that Daniel Webster gave the main speech that day, but according to Ashland historian Kay Powers, Webster wasn't even there that day. Kay Powers also assured me that *"there have been a lot of train accidents there over the years, but not so many lately."* It was also once the site of the beginning of the famous Boston Marathon, and many of the runners once stayed overnight at the inn before the race. One of the main reasons that the location of the race was changed a few years back is because one year, as the race began, a train came through separating the runners and almost permanently stopping a few of them in their tracks.

John Stone ran his inn for less than two years, but continued to own it for over 30 years. His son, Napoleon Bonaparte Stone managed the inn for many years after him. Legend is that John Stone left the running of his lucrative boarding house because he murdered a man in the basement of the building and buried the man in the dirt cellar. The victim had been a New York traveling salesman who got into a game of poker with John and his pals and accused them of cheating. In a fit of rage, John Stone supposedly hit the salesman with a heavy object (some say the butt of a pistol) and killed him. Since no one knew that the man was to stay at the inn that night, the crime was easily concealed. He was buried beneath the very table that they had been playing cards on, and he was forgotten by all but John Stone who was haunted by the angry ghost of the man forcing him to leave his beloved inn. This, of course, is all hearsay. But Raffaele Bibbo's psychics have also concluded that John Stone had killed a traveling salesman in the inn, and that is why John Stone's tortured spirit now roams the building angry at his plight, grieving for his grevious sin. Bibbo would like to dig in the cellar to see if he can find the bones of the salesman. Possibly, even the salesman still haunts the building, but Raffaele Bibbo is convinced that the main spirit of the inn is John Stone.

Upon entering the second floor main dining room of the inn both Brian and I felt the spirit of John Stone, or maybe it was of the little girl or some other ghost. But I knew instinctively that I was in the presence of something or someone supernatural. It hit me like a minor electric shock, or better explained as a major attack of pins and needles in my hands, legs, head, neck and back. Like the lyric in the song, *"That Old Black Magic,"* the moment I entered the old Victorian room, I felt *"icy fingers up and down my spine."* Brian felt the presence too, but unfortunately, Brian's reaction to ghosts is that he gets violently ill.

"I get dizzy," he explained, *"something like being seasick."*

Brian, who kept on snapping his infra-red camera, turned to me with pale lips and asked, *"Do you feel them?"*

"Yes, in this room I do," I had to admit. I hadn't had the feeling in a long time.

I sat down at one of the dining tables as Dana Seaman looked at me quizzically. I hated to admit to myself that this strange feeling I was experiencing was due to invisible beings floating about the room, but if not, what else could cause it? I tried to explain my feelings to Dana, but the more I said, the deeper his eyebrows were set in disbelief. I don't like this feeling, I told him. My mother was a highly psychic person and I probably inherited this sixth sense from her, but I wish I hadn't. He nodded, as Brian, threatening to vomit, danced about him, aiming and clicking his camera at nothing but thin air. *"This place is hot,"* Brian kept saying, *"This place is real hot."* He was snapping pictures of empty doorways, dark empty corners, paintings hanging on the walls, tables, chairs, windows, everything. Dana Seaman had to think I was weird, and had to be convinced that Brian-the-monk was a complete lunatic. He, in fact, turned the tour of the building over to manager Dennis Provencal, who had seen and heard ghosts in the inn on previous occasions and could understand or at least tolerate our antics. When we left the dining room, the pins and needles feeling left me, and Brian was no longer sick. When we returned to this dining room about an hour later, the feeling came back to me the moment I re-entered the room, but not as strongly as before. And Brian felt no nausea at all when he re-entered the upstairs dining room.

There is an unoccupied extension of the long corridor on the second floor, with rooms that have been long-empty on both sides. This leads to a window at the end of the corridor which overlooks the parking lot. While climbing into their vehicles at night many guests and employees have looked up to see a figure in the window. Some see the little girl, some see John Stone. But neither Brian nor I felt the presence of ghosts in this creepy looking corridor. Led by Dennis carrying a flashlight, we climbed a set of rickety stairs to the third floor which consisted of one large room with a creaky floor. In fact, the floorboards made so much noise that I wasn't sure that they would hold the three of us. Although the great room was cluttered with junk and shadowy figures, Brian and I got no vibes here either. As Dennis flashed the light around, he told us that the boyfriend of one of the waitresses said he saw this place all lit up one night as he came to pick her up after work.

Dennis said, *"I told him that he must mean that the second floor was all lit up, because there wasn't any electricity up there."*

"Nope," the boyfriend insisted, *"it was the third floor, blazing with lights, and some guy was up there, lookin out the window."*

From the third floor, Dennis took us down into the dirt cellar, through parts of which we had to stoop so as not to crack our heads on the beams.

"This is where most of the hauntings are," Dennis assured us as he flashed his light from one spider-webbed corner into another.

He brought us to the granite-walled secret room that was discovered by Cappy Fournier when he accidentally broke through into it in 1975, finding a cot, old blankets and a water barrel inside. Everyone concluded that it was a place to hide runaway slaves before the Civil War. Historian Kay Powers told me that Ashland was a strong Abolitionist community, and so the hideaway under the inn beside the railroad tracks was probably part of the Underground Railway. It was now partially flooded with water, so we did not enter but just peeked in. Brian, of course, flashed a couple of shots inside the room just in case one of the ghosts might be lurking there.

At the foot of the cellar stairs, down from the kitchen, a few old bedraggled chairs and a large round table sit where employees can escape, take coffee breaks and puff on cigarettes. Nearby was the freezer and ice machine, propped up by cement blocks. Brian and I lingered about the freezer but felt nothing unusual. If there were ghosts in the area, they weren't making their presence felt. Yet, it was here that bartender Butch Adams had seen the transparent figure of John Stone which petrified him so that he wouldn't enter the basement again alone.

"It was also here a few years earlier, that bartender Tony Marinaro had one hell of a scare," Dennis informed us. *"Tony was a disbeliever in ghosts, and laughed at all the stories we told him. But one night he came down here to get ice, and when he ducked his head into the freezer, something grabbed him from behind and held him there. He thought it was Kathy or Cappy fooling around at first, but when he was able to turn and look, no one was there. He then realized that it was an invisible force that held him. He broke loose and headed up the stairs. Cappy says his feet didn't hit one step on the way up. Cappy also says that he's never seen a guy so petrified. It made a believer out of Tony."*

It was here too, near the freezer, that John DuBois saw the ghost of John Stone shortly before he was hit and killed by the train, so two of the waitresses at the inn informed me.

"He saw the figure of a man down there," said one.

"It unnerved him so that he couldn't speak of much else," said the other. *"Then, only a few days after John DuBois' tragedy"* , she continued, *"Gary the waiter was in the basement and had come up to the kitchen for just a moment to get a pad of paper. When he returned below, he found the heavy table turned upside down and all the chairs were turned or thrown into another part of the cellar. Glasses that had been sitting on the table were broken, and the adding-machine that had been sitting on the table was now hanging in mid-air by its cord, attached to an overhead plug—and all this without a sound and within two or three seconds. Gary never left sight of the stairs, and no one could have gone up or down those stairs without him seeing them."*

One waitress, Jo Dallaire, who visited us while we investigated the basement, related to me, *"I was down here one Sunday night recently, and I saw the door fall off the refrigerator. And just after that happened, right before my eyes, a large oval tray that was on the freezer hit the wall, and then, like it was thrown, sailed through the air and hit me hard on the head. I saw stars and I got out of here fast."*

"But you still come down here—aren't you frightened?"

"I only come down when I have to," she replied, *"but all of us have got used to living with the ghosts in this place."*

Cappy Fournier, who isn't overly pleased that spirits haunt his establishment, has come to accept their antics and occasional disturbances. His most vivid personal experience concerning the ghosts was an argument, or one might say, a heated discussion he got into with a customer in the lounge upstairs. Steve DeSimone was there, as was Butch Adams. The customer had heard a few of the ghost stories from the boys.

"There ain't no such thing as ghosts," he shouted at Cappy. Cappy was a reluctant believer at best.

"But how else can you explain what's goin on here," he shouted back.

"If you're here Mister Ghost," shouted the patron at the ceiling very loudly, *"then show us a sign."*

Immediately there came a crackling sound and they all looked down at the table, where a heavy glass ashtray was completely and mysteriously split into equal halves. The ghosts of the John Stone Inn were making new believers out of skeptics almost every day.

When we arrived back on the first floor from our tour of the building, the lounge area was now packed with people. But the first floor dining areas were clear, so that Brian might flutter around from room to room snapping photos into the air. I sat and had a piece of squash pie as I watched him dance around Dennis like a mosquito, taking flash shots of nothing. Dennis, like Dana before him, must have thought we were really nuts. The room we were in, just off the foyer, was the one about which waitress Peggy Bache said, *"I was obliged to leave, just about this time last year at closing time. I was placing the chairs upside down on the tables, when the small linen closet door opened. I went over, closed it and latched it tightly. I then went back to stacking the chairs when the linen closet door flew open with a bang. With a shiver crawling up my spine, I walked out of the room, out the front door, and I went right home."*

"Also in this room." Dennis reported, *"Cappy was called to assist a poor woman who was dining here. She had her back to that wall, and said she felt two hands around her throat. She started screaming and almost went hysterical until Cappy calmed her down."*

It was also from this dining room that Butch Adams heard the hollow voice of a woman, as if from the grave, shout *"Nooo, help me! Please help me!"* He was at the bar at the time, and was the only mortal in the building. It's amazing that with all the experiences Butch Adams had, he remained at the inn for so long. This encounter with the voice of a woman ghost, however, is one of the few incidents that involve a female spirit other than the little girl.

Coincidentally, Ginny, one of the old managers of the inn, once removed the back of the frame that holds the only photo of John Stone. His brooding face peers out from behind the bar. *"Stuck to the back of the old photo of John Stone,"* says waitress Judy Jackson, *"Ginny found a tin print from the early 1800s. It was the photo of a little girl."*

Brian-the-monk captures the ghost of John Stone on infra-red film as he enters the first floor dining room of the Inn. The head of the ghost floats over the door, facing author Bob Cahill as he sits in the room eating squash pie. Below (insert) is a portrait of John Stone which hangs in the opposite dining room of the Inn.

Could this be a photo of the girl who haunts the inn? And what is her relationship to John Stone? According to historian Kay Powers, John Stone had only male offspring.

Upon leaving the inn late that autumn evening, I was pretty well convinced that old John Stone and a little girl who was in some way connected to him, haunted the place. A week later, when Brian showed me the photo of the ghostly head of John Stone coming through the door into the dining room where I ate my squash pie, I was convinced. The people living in and around Ashland always say, *"remember when you eat at John Stone's Inn, you never dine alone,"* and I think that's an understatement. John Stone is still running the inn!

Tin-type print of little girl dating from the last century was discovered in the frame-backing of the portrait of John Stone in the Inn. No one knows who the little girl is, but it is believed that she is the one who haunts the Inn with John Stone.

VII
Misery Islands

The islands off Manchester-by-the-Sea were my stomping grounds when I was a boy. Most boys I knew owned a boat by the age of twelve to row around the harbor in, and some like myself, saved up from odd jobs to buy a *"five-horse"* outboard motor. There are some interesting little islands in the inner bay off Beverly and Salem, but the islands we boys liked to explore and camp on were five miles out of Salem Harbor, off Manchester, known as *"The Miseries."* Big Misery, sometimes called Great Misery Island, was my favorite: over eighty acres of uninhabited woods, bushland and rocky beaches, with Stonehenge-like ruins peppering the landscape. As you enter Casino Cove, some two miles off the coast of Manchester, high up on a hill to the right are rock and brick ruins, looking to a boy like the remnants of Dracula's Castle. They are actually the ruins of a hotel called *"The Casino,"* which was destroyed in a mysterious fire in 1926, as were the few summer homes that once dotted the island. I was told that over 100 people once lived on the island, but when I was twelve, the island was mine and mine alone.

During week long summer camping trips, we boys, usually eight or more in number, would occupy the island and play games on it all day long, every day, occasionally stopping to fish for supper. At night by the campfire, the ghost stories, told one right after the other, were enough to freeze one permanently to the rock or stump one was sitting on to listen. There were rats on the island too, big red-eyed water-rats that didn't fear humans, and they would often enter camp late at night, just as the ghost stories were running out—and they would send us scurrying into out tents in climactic terror—Oh, What wonderful times those were!

Hugging Big Misery, on the opposite end of the island from Casino Cove, is Little Misery Island, one-twentieth the size of her big sister. In the narrow saltwater cove separating the islands lies the splintered, rusted hull of a shipwreck, barely visible today. She was once the great steamer *"City of Rockland,"* that wrecked and burned in a blinding snowstorm in 1905. We would often pitch our tents on the little island near the wreck and catch baby squid after the turn of the tide in the rusty hull, excellent bait for cod and flounder fishing. On foggy nights out there, the foghorn from nearby Baker's Island would blare at intervals of thirty seconds, keeping even the seagulls awake. We wondered aloud if we should row or motor across the deep water channel to Baker's and dismantle or possibly sink the foghorn. Although Baker's Island was less than a mile away, we would never visit there. We wouldn't think of even going near that island. It is some sixty acres of woods, brush and granite,

Lightning strikes "The Miseries." The center lightning bolt is striking the Baker's Island lighthouse; the right bolt hits near the haunted Wells Cottage; and the left bolt hits Little Misery Island. Photo by Norman "Dugie" Russell.

The old Coast Guard complex at Baker's Island, with the lighthouse in the background. The haunted waterpump is just to the right of this photo.

has a lovely white lighthouse on it, and some sixty summer cottages. Baker's was then, and still is, the only inhabited island of some fifteen islands in Salem Bay, but when we were boys, we weren't interested in islands that had people on them. Baker's stands in a line with the two Miseries, as if protecting the entrance to the bay, with Cape Ann slicing off and out to sea on the left, and Halfway Rock, like some pre-historic obelisk, facing the island as the last bastion before Europe. The three island chain is called by sailors, as one faces them heading to sea, *"Big Misery, Little Misery, and Great Misery,"* or just, *"The Miseries."* Noted poet James Russell Lowell called them *"the true islands of the sirens."*

I didn't visit Baker's Island until I was 54 years old, and then, only seven months after I had undergone my second open-heart surgery. It was in April of 1989 and my niece Patty, my brother Jim's third of four daughters, was caretaker of the island and had been for over two years. She remained alone on the island during the winter months to care for the sixty empty cottages, keep an eye on the lighthouse, and make any needed repairs. Patty is an artist, and during her spare time she painted island scenes in oils. I was amazed that she could remain for months alone on an island, even if it was only a few miles from the mainland, and especially amidst all those empty homes—like living in a ghost town. Obviously, I concluded, there must be a haunted house among them. Patty, or *"Trish"* as her friends call her, isn't one to be frightened off by ghosts. As she says, *"I defy them by ignoring them."* She did, however, lead me to believe that mysterious things were happening on Baker's Island, especially while the residents were away, and that if Brian-the monk and I wished to visit and spend a night or two, we were welcome. Brian and I decided to do just that, but first I wanted to talk to previous island caretakers who had since moved back to the mainland and had informed others that they had encountered ghosts on Baker's.

Andy Jerome, who left the island to become Harbormaster of Danvers, Massachusetts, had been caretaker with his wife Ruth for four years prior to Patty taking over. In meeting Andy, he immediately told me that he thought the island foghorn was haunted. I had to laugh at this, for it certainly had kept me awake a few nights in my youth. *"The foghorn would go on for no reason, on crystal clear nights,"* said Andy. *"I had to walk almost across the island from the caretaker's quarters to the lighthouse, where the horn was locked up, to shut it off. Every time I got right to the door of the building where it was blaring away, it would stop. This happened more than a dozen times each winter, and it would always stop just before I entered the little building behind the lighthouse where it is housed. I'm talking about cold nights, sometimes below zero, when there wasn't a cloud in the sky, nor a patch of fog around to set off the sensor. It was like the foghorn got lonely and wanted company, but all it needed was to see me at the door and it was comforted. The Coast Guard would inevitably send repairmen out to fix the horn and would find nothing wrong, with no explanation as to why it sounded."*

History reveals that the old lighthouse keeper, Walter Rogers, had similar problems with the island's fogbell as Jerome did with the foghorn. Prior to a fogsiren being installed in 1906, a loud fogbell, operated by an automatic mechanism, was located on the rocks below the lighthouse. It once clanked loudly every half minute for 72 hours without a hitch, but it was hit by lightning on August 1, 1877 and never ran right again. It was replaced, but the new mechanism kept failing, which forced keeper Rogers to leave his post in the lighthouse and spend hours in the damp fog banging the bell with a hammer. On July 16 of 1879, the bell tower was once again demolished by a bolt of lightning and was replaced by a third bell. But this one was even more temperamental, being instrumental, some islanders say, in having Rogers leave his post as lighthouse keeper within two years. Seventeen years after Rogers retired his post, on July 4, 1898, he came back to Baker's Island for a picnic. With 60 others he left the island in late afternoon aboard the steamer *"Surf City."* Those remaining on the island could not understand why the fogbell started ringing automatically as the steamer left for the mainland. Approaching Beverly Harbor, a great Waterspout stormed out of the sea, lifted the *"Surf City"* out of the water and turned her bottoms-up, sinking her within seconds. Eight people died. Walter Rogers miraculously survived.

"That whole area including the lighthouse, the little foghorn building, and the adjacent white Coast Guard houses, is haunted," says Ruth Jerome, Andy's wife. *"And these are the only buildings with electricity on the island. Every time I had to walk over to that part of the island, it raised the hackles on the back of my neck. It's like there is some kind of a presence there. It wasn't that I was afraid to go over there, 'cause I wasn't, but it did give me a creepy feeling. I never felt frightened when I was alone out there, but I never felt alone either, if you know what I mean.*

I'm as skeptical about this kind of thing as your niece Patty is," said Ruth, *"but things just happen out there that can't be explained. Andy and I would see kerosene lamps on in the little general -store, and this is in the winter when the store was shut down and nobody else was on the island, We'd see the lights every once in awhile, usually around dusk, so others we told this to, said it was the reflection of the setting sun on the windows, but we knew it wasn't. Things would move out there too—you put a tool or a bucket down here and it ends up there, and you know it wasn't you that moved it, and there is no one else around to move things on you. Wheelbarrows that are used to deliver goods and groceries to the cottages from the dock and store, would end up on the other side of the island. Big plumbing wrenches, ladders, and especially plastic buckets which are used to carry water from the wells and pumps and pond, just*

86

disappear from under your nose, or move long distances in a matter of seconds. At first Andy and I thought we were going crazy, but then we'd just have to blame the ghosts—there was no other explanation. Then there was that terrifying experience at the Chase Cottage that chills me even to this day....

It was the second winter we were there and it was an exceptionally mild evening in December. Andy and I were making our rounds about dusk, checking out all the cottages, and on the east side, facing the open sea, when we came to the big old rambling cottage owned by the Chase family of Ipswich, we heard voices coming from inside. Most of the windows were boarded up for the winter and the door was locked, so my initial thought was that Martha, one of the Chase girls, had sailed out to the island with friends to have a party. Andy and I could clearly hear the clinking of glasses, low muffled conversation and music. We knocked on the door, but there was no answer from inside, yet the party seemed to continue on. Andy and I circled the house on the porch. There was one window not boarded up. I placed my face to the window, cupped my hands to block out the fading sunlight and looked in. I saw a kerosene chandelier-light flaming its brilliance and the shadowy movement of people within the room, but the window was dusty and warped, so I couldn't discern who the people were. Andy and I concluded, since they wouldn't answer the door nor our shouts of 'hello,' they were intruders from the mainland, possibly a bunch of kids out for a lark. We had passkeys to all the cottages, which we carried with us on our rounds, so we entered the cottage, and were utterly shocked to find it empty—not a person inside. We just couldn't believe it. Both Andy and I heard and saw through the window, people having a party. I could tell Andy was really spooked and I was too. By the time we had searched the entire cottage and locked it up again, it was dark out and we walked back to our caretakers quarters above the social hall on the west side of the island, but that evening we walked across the island a lot quicker than usual, and I must say, I had a hard time sleeping that night."

The interview with the Jeromes stimulated my interest, but my follow-up call to the Moores of Manchester, caretakers for five years prior to the Jeromes, convinced me that Baker's Island was a hotspot of ghostly activity. As with the Jeromes, the female caretaker had more to say than her male partner. I hadn't mentioned the Jerome experience at the Chase Cottage to the Moores, but Barbara Moore immediately told me that her most frightening experience on the island had been at the Chase Cottage. Barbara was living over the social hall, where the caretakers are provided quarters and she was preparing dinner. Carl, her husband, was off the island, visiting the mainland, and nobody was on the island but her.

"It was a clear windless day in February," she told me, *"about dusk. I needed a spice if I remember right,"* she said, *"and I decided to go to the family*

cottage on the East side of the island to get it, before darkness set in. I decided to take a shortcut to 'Calamity Hill,' as the Chase's call it, through their backyard. I at first only heard a babel of voices coming from the house, but I knew that no one could be inside, and the cottage was all boarded up. There was a light snow covering the ground and there were no telltale footprints to the cottage. Then I heard faint music, but I couldn't make out the tune. I knew it wasn't noise coming across the water from the mainland, which can happen if the wind is right, but there was no wind, and the sounds were definitely coming from the big old house. It sounded like a party was going on inside. As I got closer to the house, the sounds got louder. I finally stopped in my tracks, turned and ran back to my place. I grabbed the shotgun, loaded it and sat by the door. I was so frightened that when my dog came scratching at the door to let her in, I came close to shooting her. I knew those weren't really people in the Chase House, and that only meant that they were ghosts. Carl didn't come back to the island from the mainland until late that night, and I didn't sleep a wink."

Barbara Moore also informed me that two of the Chase girls, who lived in the cottage every summer from the time they were little girls, had mentioned to her at one time that they too had weird experiences at the cottage.

"If I recall," said Barbara, *"one of them saw a ghost up in the attic."*

I tracked down Martha Chase, now Martha Krauser, living in Malden, Massachusetts.

"Yes" she said, *"I heard the spirits in the house, but I never saw them. My sister Pam did, in my grandmother's bedroom on the third floor. The stairway to the third floor, I always considered haunted. There was a presence up there. When I was just out of my teens, I'd often go out to the island in late autumn, when no one was there but the caretakers, and I'd stay alone in the house, but I'd avoid the third floor. Sometimes in the late afternoon or early evening when it was quiet with no wind blowing, I'd hear voices in the house, so low that you couldn't make out what they were saying, and I heard a slight strain of music. Now that I think of it, I heard glasses clinking too,"* said Martha. *"It was not a normal sound and it was very unsettling. It only happened to me about four times in all the years I was out there, and always in the off-season, when everyone else was gone."*

Martha's sister, Pam Chase, confirmed seeing the ghost of a man in the attic.

"I was only ten years old at the time," says Pam, who lives in Beverly, *"and I was sleeping on the third floor, in what we called 'the blue room.' I woke up in the early morning, just before dawn. It was about 4 A.M. A strange looking man was standing at the foot of my bed. He wore an old khaki-green army jacket, but he was transparent and obviously a ghost. I was petrified and pulled the blanket over my head and shouted for him to go away. When I lifted the blanket and peeked out, he was gone and the sun was coming up."*

The Chase girls further convinced me that there were lively spirits whooping it up on Baker's Island, and especially at the Chase Cottage but usually, it seems, when vacationers had left the island for the season. Patty didn't have a phone on the island, so I contacted her via marine radio, through my brother Jim who was the Salem Harbormaster. She picked up Brian and me at Manchester, along with her sister Cheryl and Cheryl's eight-year old daughter, Heather, and transported us to the island in her Boston Whaler. We were all staying overnight, and it was a night we were all to remember.

Although Baker's Island is owned by the City of Salem, it is mostly private property. The only truly safe landing place on the island is the long pier that juts out from the west end, but it, too, with its iron stairs and moving platform without a float provides difficult footing when the sea is rough. In a squall or even slight storm, it's almost impossible to land on Baker's Island. Brian-the-monk, with all his ghost-hunting equipment, almost ended up in the icy seas that cold April morning when we arrived at the pier. Patty, the trusty and capable sailor that she is, maneuvered us in successfully under the pier and Brian leapt for the stairs with infra-red binoculars and camera swinging from his neck. As he landed on shaky limbs, a large swell rose up and covered him to his knees, and then it receded. For the next two days, his shoes squeaked loudly when he walked.

"You have to time your jump to the pier platform," Patty said from the stern of the whaler, *"make your move just after the swell crests."*

Following Patty's advice, which came too late for Brian, we all made it safely ashore without getting wet. We then carried our gear to nearby Burnham Hall, where the islanders have their socials, dances, and summer gatherings. We were all to stay upstairs in the caretaker's quarters, which were lighted and heated by their own generator. Patty said that the islanders could have opted for electricity in 1938 when an underwater cable was layed to the light-house from Manchester and provided the 'juice' for the lighthouse and the two Coast Guard houses next door to it, but the others voted to outlaw such a modern convenience. The light was automated in 1972, but the islanders continued to reject electricity.

I found the island to be uniquely interesting and scenic. Head-high sumac trees with red leaves cover the island in many little clusters, looking like giant poinsettia flowers, and shiny-leaved poison ivy clings to many of the seaside boulders. I was made aware of poison sumac and ivy as a boy exploring the islands, for I suffered greatly from its juices, often scratching the rashes it produced well into the winter months. Wild blackberry and raspberry bushes were in abundance, another lure to these islands for young boys in late summer and early autumn when the fruit is ripe. Briar patches, ferns and tall marsh grass seem to dominate the land near the little ponds at the center of the island, where a myriad of dirt paths interconnect, leading off in every direction to the hodgepodge of cottages scattered all over the island. Some of the cottages that crowd the cliffs and pebbly beaches of the circular island, look like they might fall down in a strong breeze, but most are sturdy and as picturesque as might be found on a lazy back street of Manchester-by-the-Sea. Almost all have porches of one sort or another, and most seemed in some stage of disrepair. Surprisingly, any grass around the cottages was mowed and clipped, and all gardens, be they vegetable or flower, were well-groomed.

Wild roses grew proliferously and grapevines were located here and there along the narrow paths, so visitors and islanders might pick and snack while traveling from one quaint cottage to another. There were occasional shadowy glens of small evergreens and knarly crabapple trees, looking to me like little enchanted forests were elves and leprechauns might hold their annual picnic. There was the constant squeaking of seagulls as we walked along, the sound of breakers crashing over the rocks on the seaward side, and pebbles clacking and scraping on the beaches at bayside. There was also the odor of wood burning in the air, reminding me much of the smell of peatfires in Ireland. Fire, of course, is the greatest fear of all the islanders, but most of the cottages have fireplaces, and as early as April, four or five islanders had arrived to open their cottages and were burning out the chill and dampness of winter.

As we walked the island I felt like I stepped back in history. There was no sound, sight, or smell of vehicles, no pavement or telephone poles, just meandering trails going from one simple cottage to the next, and many of the cottages weren't locked.

"You don't need locks out here," Patty chuckled at my surprise, *"everyone's home is open to his neighbor. Little islands never have thieves,"* said Patty, *"because they are too easily detected and captured."*

In the few cottages we entered, I was amazed at the old yet fine and sturdy furniture they held. *"These are truly antiques,"* I said aloud and she chuckled again.

"When you buy a house out here, you always buy it furnished," she said *"cause nobody is going to start lugging heavy furniture on or off this island, it's too much of a chore. The furniture in these cottages has been here since the cottages were built, and quite a few of them were built in the last century. The old stuff that was thrown away fifty years ago on the mainland is still holding up fine out here—it has to."*

I was especially intrigued with the old gas and kerosene chandeliers and oil lamps, something I hadn't seen during fifty-plus years of living on the mainland only a few miles away, but were necessities of life in every home out here on the island. Each home also displayed lightning rods, another necessity out here. The lighthouse is constantly being hit by lightning and cottages on the high ground are often hit. In 1930, islander Louis Swett was sitting in his cottage reading the newspaper when a bolt of lightning came down his chimney and killed him. A few years later his cottage was torn down by the family. Lightning has been known to start fires on the island, the residents' greatest fear. There are rainbarrells outside each cottage to collect water so it is always available to douse a fire before it spreads,.and flexible water pipes with hydrants leading form the duck pond are located throughout the island. There is a little firehouse beside the pond housing an old watercart and other firefighting equipment, and firedrills are held periodically by the islanders during the summer months.

"When the big bell is rung outside the hall," said Patty, *"that means that there is an emergency and all must assemble at the hall. There used to be a big hotel out here, with 75 rooms in it, built in the last century, but it burnt to the ground in 1906, probably due to some careless smoker."*

As we passed the lighthouse, three islanders came out of one of the white Coast Guard houses to join us in our walk. Ruth Buck, who owned one of the houses with electricity in it, assured me that the surges of electricity left over from what was needed to keep the lighthouse shining, were usually enough to keep one bulb flickering, a radio tuned, or allow a grainy black and white picture on a color TV set. I told Ruth I had heard that her house was haunted.

"Probably is," she replied, *"but I've been living here so long, I don't notice."* The two teenaged boys with Ruth perked up when I said *"haunted,"* not with fear but with enthusiasm.

"That house right over there," said young Devin Gardner, pointing to a little white cottage sitting in the grass away from the rocky shore, *"is truly haunted."*

"That's the old Pilot Retreat," said Ruth. Patty had introduced Ruth as the island historian, so I asked her to tell me more. *"It was built in 1848, the oldest cottage on the island. It was where the pilots lived in the last century. Their job was to spot the clipper ships coming into Salem and guide them in."*

A ghostly tale told around the island campfires, and told to me by teenager Brenna Collins, is that *"The old Pilot would spot a clipper and row out to guide it in, but one foggy night when he rowed back after guiding the ship into the harbor, he got lost in the fog, and never returned to the Pilot House. On foggy nights,"* says Brenna, *"you can hear the sound of his oars splashing in the water, then the scraping of his row boat on the pebbles, and his footsteps in the sand, and he's been seen coming ashore, but he never quite makes it back home."*

Her pal Kelly Smith, who lives with his family in the Pilot House during the summer, assured me that he had never seen the ghost of the pilot, but he wished he had.

"Every cottage out here has a reputation of one sort or another," said Patty, *"and because it gets pretty spooky out here at night without electricity, ghost stories abound. A horse died over there by the lighthouse, and at night people*

hear the horse whinnying. There's another story about a thief who stole a fortune in jewels from a Manchester mansion and was caught hiding out in one of the cottages, but when he was captured he didn't have the jewels with him. He went to Salem Jail and died behind bars a few years later, but on nights of a full moon, his ghost has been seen sneaking around in the shadows, searching for his hidden bag of jewels. There's another about a woman who came out here to visit with her husband, but during the day, while walking near the marsh, she got lost, and although her husband returned to the cottage they were visiting, she never did. She is dressed in white, from ankles to bonnet, and is seen still hectically walking the paths late at night to find the cottage, and those who have spotted her say that her feet are moving faster than she is...I'm telling you Uncle Bob," Patty smiled up at me, *"the ghost stories are endless."*

"Those are tales," I corrected her. *"I'm looking for true stories, and that's why I want to visit the Chase Cottage at dusk. Maybe Brian can get photos of the spirited party that seems to go on there now and then—that's a real ghost story!"*

"They call that house the 'Party House' now," said Patty. *"And right next to it is another that is said to be haunted—I just hope Brian has enough film."*

She giggled and walked on along the crest of the hill on the east side of the island, overlooking the open sea and Halfwalk Rock. We now looked like a string of mountain climbers, nine of us in all: Patty, Ruth, the two island boys, Cheryl, Heather, Cheryl's friend Barb Zwiercan, who had sailed out that morning to be in the ghost hunt, Brian and me—enough to frighten off any island ghost who obviously would be accustomed to peace and quiet and adverse to such crowds.

As we walked along the east shore, I asked Ruth Buck what she and others did for excitement out here every summer.

"We sit on rocking chairs on the porch; we watch the clouds and we watch the birds. We have a great horned owl that lives out here, and she takes up much of our attention." She pointed to a large grey cottage sitting on a slope near the rocky shore. It looked almost new. *"There was a Quonset hut sitting here just after World War II,"* she informed me. *"The workmen building this house lived in it, and used to go out at night to rob lobster traps. One night, one of them swam out to lift a trap and steal lobsters from it, but he never came back."*

Patty then informed me that the woman who lived in the Quonset hut every summer, Naomi Thresher Colyer, was an avid athlete. She would swim off the rocks every morning, often visiting the lobster boat fishermen as they pulled their traps and she would buy lobsters from them to bring back to the island for breakfast. On the morning of August 20, 1961, Mrs. Colyer didn't make it back to shore with her lobsters.

"I was there when her little girl ran up to the lighthouse to tell the Coast

Guard keeper that her mother didn't return from her swim," said Ruth. *"We called the Salem Coast Guard station, and a helicopter was flying over the Quonset hut before we could even get down here. They found her body floating on the surface."*

"Undertow?" I asked.

"I don't know," said Ruth, *"just another drowning, but the Quonset hut didn't last long after that—it was torn down."*

"I heard that the workmen building this place wouldn't live in the Quonset hut after the drowning," said Patty.

"So, that's how you take care of ghosts out here," I said to both of them, *"you tear down their living quarters."*

"But apparently Naomi kept coming round," said Patty, giving Ruth a knowing sideglance.

"Mister Collins has seen the ghost of Naomi at the water pump," interjected one of the teenagers, a boy named Ben Fabry. *"Also Mister Scott from the Lucas cottage heard the pump handle squeaking in the middle of the night, got out of bed, looked outside, and saw her ghost, still dripping wet, wearing a bathingsuit, pumping water."*

"Baloney," said Patty.

I knew, however, that young Fabry was right about Bruce Collins, for he told me in a conversation I had with him earlier, that he had a hair-raising experience at the pump.

"It was about ten o'clock at night, just after the drowning," said Collins, *"and I was walking home alone to my cottage. As I passed the pump over by the lighthouse, I heard a clunk, and then saw a shadow place a milk can at the pump to draw water. The milk can was immediately familiar, for it was the one Naomi always used to carry her water. It was quite distinctive, and she was the only one who used a milk can. I looked back and saw the handle pumping, but saw no human hand making it move, so I took off down the path, lickity-split, and I didn't look back again."*

It was late afternoon when we arrived at *"Calamity Hill"* and the Chase Cottage. It was a large rambling place, stark and quite spooky-looking in the fading sunlight. We all entered the house, first listening for muted voices, music and the clinking of glasses. Brian immediately headed for the upper floors of the shadowy interior, as excited as a kid in a candy store. I sat in the large gloomy living room with Patty and Ruth as Brian and the young folks rumbled from room to room above us. The youngsters followed Brian as if he were the pied-piper. Brian kept talking to them, and he called to spirits as he clicked his camera, we could hear him distinctly from the main floor. It was such a bedlam that I would think any resident ghost would be frightened out of its wits. Brian spent about ten minutes upstairs and then returned to us with the kids following close behind.

"*I feel nothing in here,*" he said to me with disappointment.

"*Me neither,*" I said, "*but it certainly has a nice ghostly atmosphere.*"

Patty said that right next door was a cottage facing the one we were in called "*The Ghost House,*" by some, but she didn't have the key to it. Brian was disappointed again, as was I , but only because Patty didn't know why it was called "*The Ghost House.*"

"*There are others,*" she smiled at Brian and me, sensing our disappointment.

Outside, she walked behind "*The Ghost House,*" and down a slippery little path to an embankment facing the rocks and open sea, where two little cottages sat side by side with but a few feet between them. She headed for the furthest one that had a roofed-in porch with classic arched breezeways.

"*This house was vacant and boarded up when I was a girl on the island,*" said Ruth.

"*An old lady use to live here,*" said Devin Gardner "*She'd move into her house in the beginning of summer and we'd never see her again 'til fall, when she'd move out.*"

"*That's Katharine Wells Leffler,*" said Patty. "*She's too old to come out here now. She was one of the organizers of the U.S.O. during World War II, and for fifteen years was delegate to the World Federation of Mental Health. She was really quite a gal, but she had no one, she has outlived all in her family. Her parents died, her husband too, so she'd come out here by herself and spend the entire summer. Her folks bought this place for her little sister Winifred, who suffered from severe diabetes, but she died before she could make it to the island. This is a real old house too,*" she said, unlocking the door, "*it was built in 1896.*"

When I entered the house, I got that old pins and needles sensation down my spine. At first I thought I experienced that feeling because the interior reminded me of houses I lived in or entered when I was a boy. The furniture was all 1930s, and only 1930s magazines and other items were laying about.

"*Nothing in this cottage has been moved since before 1934,*" said Ruth. "*Katharine who is now in her late eighties, insists her home here stay as it was the last day her parents were here. When she visits she touches nothing and sleeps on a cot in the corner of one room of the first floor.*"

"*I thought you and Brian might want to stay overnight here,*" said Patty, an elfish twinkle in her eye.

"*I'd love to,*" said Brian, looking at me like I was about to announce a trip to Disney World to a child.

"*I wouldn't stay overnight in this cottage if you paid me.*"

"*Why not?*" demanded Brian.

"*Because it's too spooky,*" I replied, "*and don't even try to change my mind.*"

The Old Pilot Retreat, built in 1846, where clipper-ship pilots once lived. Legend is that old Joe Perkins left this house one evening to escort a ship into harbor but never returned. His ghost can be seen and heard rowing ashore to the island on foggy nights.

The Baker's Island Fire Department: Islanders Ruth Buck, Ben Fabry and Devin Gardner are always ready to rush to the fire hut located next to the island pond, where the fire-fighting equipment is kept. Fire is the islanders greatest fear, but ghosts are a close second.

Island caretaker Patty Taft, stands outside the Chase Cottage, where ghosts gather behind the boarded windows in off-season to party. Usually about dusk is when they raise the devil.

On the rocky seaward coast of Baker's Island is the Wells Cottage (right), where furniture and other articles inside have not been moved or touched since the early 1930s. A carpenter recently hired to do repair work inside the cottage was kissed by the ghost—he ran from the cottage and refused to return.

The cottage was, however, fascinating. Cheryl and the others kept picking up packages and canned goods and reading the labels out loud. Barb Zwiercan called us into one room to show us an antique washing machine, and Brian insisted we join him in the third floor bedroom to see the antiques on display there—old trunks, chamber pots and umbrella stands. It was like a museum, each room I entered bringing back fond memories of the past, until I got to the kitchen. Following close behind me was young Devin Gardner. He propped himself sitting on a shelf as I bent down to look out a low window that faced the porch and open sea. A strong feeling of depression immediately enveloped me. I knew it was not my own depression, but something, some force unseen, trying to overpower me from without. I stayed in my stooped position staring at the sea and Halfway Rock beyond, allowing the feeling to penetrate my being, but when it started overwhelming me, I stepped back from the window and it subsided.

Devin realized that something was happening to me and got down from his perch. *"There certainly is something haunting at that window,"* I told him and tried to explain the depression that had flooded my mind and body. He left the room quickly. I stepped into the space again, stooped down and looked out the window, and again a deep depression enveloped me and increased in intensity as I tried to fight it off. The depression, I knew, wasn't mine, and it wasn't the sight of heavy swells on the sea, for I had seen them many times before in my life. It was some unseen and unknown force by that window that was trying to capture me, and I could not understand how or why it was happening. Again, I backed away from the window and the feeling subsided. Patty was now in the room, fetched by Devin.

"There is a great sadness in this house," I said to her, *"a very great sadness."* At that moment the house seemed to tremble on its foundation. We heard Brian shout from the third floor,

"Everyone out of this house, there are bad spirits in here." He came tumbling down the stairs with Heather and Cheryl screaming at his heels, and they all headed out the front door. Heather was in tears and Cheryl had turned a pasty white. The rest of us were out the door right behind them.

"What did you see?" I asked Brian.

"A great black beast," he announced matter-of-factly. *"I will come back tonight with my holy water. This is an evil place."*

Outside the wind was howling, the sun was setting and the nearby surf was pounding the rocks. We all stood outside on the bluff staring at the house like it was some living thing. As far as I was concerned, this was a real haunted house. I discovered when we returned to our living quarters over Burnham Hall, that Patty had purposely brought us to this cottage, for she too had had a strange experience there a year before.

"It was late fall and I was all alone on the island," said Patty. *"I was on the Wells Cottage arched porch, and I was painting a canvas of the sea. As you*

97

know I'm not a believer of ghosts and such things, and feel that there must be an explanation for all these so-called hauntings. It was late afternoon and I was deep into my work, when I heard a banging coming from the house. At first I thought it was a window shutter, but then I realized that the banging wasn't in tune with the wind. It wasn't a rhythmic pounding and it was coming from inside the house. Thinking that someone might be inside the cottage, I began backing off the porch with my paints and canvas. I looked up and saw the curtains in the second floor front window waving frantically, and then they stopped; then the curtains in another window started waving—not slight movement, but heavy fluttering—like someone was tugging at them. I was backing up the embankment now, ready to drop my gear and run like hell, especially when I saw a large black hand come around the curtain and start slapping at the window from the inside, as if beckoning me to come in. If I had let my imagination take over at that point, I would have been back at the pier in a flash and rowing to Manchester, but I watched the black hand, which slowly but surely transformed into feathers—it was the wing of a big black bird. Birds periodically fly down chimneys out here, so I was relieved. I got out my keys, unlocked the front door and entered the cottage to retrieve the bird. The birds usually fight and bite when I try to capture them, so I wrapped my hand in an old sweatshirt to protect it, but when I reached for the bird, which was just sitting on the windowsill when I entered the house, it didn't fight at all, but just allowed me to pick it up and take it outside.

That over, I began painting again, but it wasn't twenty minutes later, the banging started again and the curtain was waving. Sure enough, it was the same bird, or at least it looked like the same bird, and it allowed me to pick it up and release it outside. Less than ten minutes later, it was back inside again. Now I was getting angry, for it was interrupting my work, but the third time I entered the cottage to save the bird, the atmosphere inside seemed to have changed. Maybe it was because dusk was approaching, I don't know, but I had this ominous feeling. It was much like what you said you felt—a chilling depression. Even the bird was nastier and tried to nip me when I grabbed it. I left the cottage and the porch that day feeling quite differently about the place. When I had first come to the island I felt drawn to the Wells place and especially their arched porch sitting right on the sea, but after the bird incident I felt like the house was trying to possess me. And that's why I wanted to bring you and Brian there before I told you of my experience, to see if you would find anything haunting about the place."

"Anything else you haven't told me?" I asked.

"Just a couple of more things," she smiled coyly. "A couple of years back, a few of the islanders hired a carpenter to modernize the kitchen in the Wells Cottage. They wanted to surprise old Katharine before she came out to live there for the summer. Her stove was outdated and didn't work, and the place was *dysfunctional. In fact nothing in the kitchen worked. But, the carpenter lasted only a couple of days and refused to go back into the cottage again. The reason, so I was told by the islanders who hired him, is that he was kissed by a ghost in the kitchen of the house, full mouthed, right on the lips—and he bolted, never to return. John Taft, who, as you know, became my husband a few months ago, took that carpenter's place, but when Katharine arrived on the island, she was upset that they had attempted to update her kitchen and insisted that no more work be done. Maybe she knows who the ghost is, her mother or sister, perhaps. There was, by the way, a small table and chair by the window where you had your experience,"* said Patty.

I asked John Taft if he had any strange experiences while working in the Wells Cottage. John, a quiet, thoughtful man, paused before answering, nodded slightly to Patty and said.

"Why do you think I worked so late down there and always came home with a smile on my face?"

Obviously John didn't have any haunting experiences while working in the Wells Cottage, but he and Patty did encounter one mystery concerning the cottage. Twice in the winter, after new snow had fallen on the island, they found enormous animal tracks down by the arched porch of the Wells Cottage.

"They looked like the pawprints of some giant rabbit," said John.

"And we couldn't tell if it was a two-legged or four-legged creature," said Patty. There are no large animals known to live on the island, but there are wild rabbits, racoons and skunks, and, of course, the ever-present red-eyed rats, as big as cats.

"These tracks were almost as big as my feet," said Patty, *"and just seeing them made me nervous, but neither John nor I could figure out what kind of an animal would leave them. We also found similar tracks by the store."*

Maybe this black, misty beast that Brian felt he saw on the third floor of the cottage had left its footprints in the snow. My feeling, however, was that the power that tried to depress me in the kitchen, was female. I was certainly glad it hadn't tried to kiss me as it kissed the carpenter and whatever it was, woman or beast, I was convinced, as was Brian, that the Wells cottage was haunted. I decided not to tell Brian about the kissed carpenter or the foot-prints in the snow. He was determined to go back to the cottage that night, but since I was just recuperating from my second open-heart surgery, and had become quite cowardly about the Wells Cottage, I refused to join him. I had been walking the island all day and needed rest. Besides, all the others wanted to join Brian, and I felt it would be a fiasco.

Cheryl was determined to go back at night, as were the two boys, Ben and Devin. Patty would show them the way back to the cottage, but the rest of us would remain upstairs in Burnham Hall. I was to sleep on the porch that night, so I made my bed early under the stars and heard Brian and his followers head out with their flashlights, infra-red camera and binoculars. It's awful to get old and infirm I said to myself as I heard them disappear into the blackness, but sometimes it can be a blessing in disguise, for I had no desire to return to the Wells Cottage.

They were gone for two hours and I was still awake when they returned, all whispering loudly, their voices filled with excitement. My niece Cheryl insisted on steering me from the porch to the living quarters to hear her story: When the gang of them had reached the Party House, Patty insisted that Brian be allowed to go to the Wells Cottage alone. Patty realized that Brian was being distracted by too many followers. Cheryl, who's older than Patty, insisted on joining Brian. As Patty and the teenagers sat on the bluff by the Party House, overlooking the rocky perimeter and under a bright moon, they watched Brian and Cheryl enter the arched porch, Cheryl with the infra-red binoculars and Brian with the camera.

"At first, I only saw cloud-like forms at the end of the porch, by the kitchen window," said Cheryl, still nervous as she told me her story. *"There were three dark shapes. I had never seen things like this before, yet I wasn't fearful. I shouted to Brian that I could see these ghost-like forms through his binoculars and that they were moving toward us. Brian seemed to get awfully nervous about them. He, I assumed, could see them too through his camera, but he later told me he couldn't. The camera takes infra-red photos, but he doesn't see the energy. He wasn't taking photos. He had taken out his bottle of holy water and was splashing it about. He shouted to me to watch the figures through the binoculars, which I did, and the holy water made them retreat back to the corner of the porch."*

I knew that Brian seldom went out ghost-hunting without holy water, a religious relic, or his rosary, but to have Cheryl as a witness to the reactions of spirits when sprinkled with holy water was truly enlightening. Cheryl had always been imaginative and enthusiastic since she was a child, but I knew that what she was saying was the truth as she saw it and that she wasn't exaggerating.

"The figures slowly returned and I watched them. They looked like grey bubbles, but they were in human form. Brian seemed afraid of them, yet they seemed playful to me, until they started swarming about me like a pack of bees. Brian sprayed them again and they dispersed. Brian then asked me to scan the porch with the glasses, to look for something else, but he didn't say what. Then I saw it, standing in the semi-darkness by one of the arches—a great black figure, like a huge animal, and I was overwhelmed with foreboding. I shouted to Brian that I saw this great blob, this terrible thing, standing on the side as if watching us, ready to pounce. Brian turned and splashed holy water where I was pointing,

and this black thing moved. When it did, this stifling, crushing feeling came over me. I almost felt like I couldn't breathe. It moved slowly, but away from us and up, towards the second floor. It was like a tornado, black and terrible, and it moved like it was anchored with chains to the house. It thoroughly scared me, and I'm pretty sure it frightened Brian, too, for he had us back off the porch, the holy water bottle firmly grasped in his hand, ready to sprinkle wherever I pointed. The earlier grayer images or spirits seemed female and spritey, but not fearful. This evil black thing, I felt was male and quite dangerous. It was like death itself."

Brian seemed exhausted and had little to say but..., *"I had a feeling of foreboding when I left here tonight, and now I know it was real."*

Patty, who might normally conclude that Brian and Cheryl were letting their fears control their senses, was mystified by what she, Ben and Dennis saw while they were on the porch surrounded by evil spirits. The seagulls who usually sit quietly on the rocks surrounding the cottage, were stirred into abnormal activity.

"They just went berserk," said Patty, *"for no reason. Hundreds of them started spinning around the cottage, squawking and screeching, yet Cheryl and Brian hadn't disturbed them, and neither had I or the boys. I have been near the rocks in this area many times before, night and day, and I've never seen the gulls react like that before. You know me, Uncle Bob, I don't get spooked easy, but something was certainly going on that I just don't understand."*

"I feel like I stepped into another dimension," concluded Cheryl. *"It was like desolation. I'm now convinced there are other unseen worlds besides our own existing right here around us, and they've always been here. The one I saw tonight, I don't like, but it will get me to church next Sunday."*

When I returned to the mainland I had another startling discovery. My daughter Keri had visited Patty on the island for a few days, some two months earlier.

"Did you go to the old Wells Cottage?" she asked me before I could tell her my story. *"I never said anything to Patty,"* she said, *"because Patty loves the place so, but I think it's haunted. I had a terrible depressing feeling overcome me in the kitchen of that house...."*

"By the kitchen window?" I asked.

"Yes, how'd you know?" she replied. *"It happened when I was sitting by the kitchen window, looking out to sea."*

Keri's revelation was the convincer for me—the Wells Cottage definitely held unhappy spirits. But were these merely emotions experienced in the past by a living being that remained there by the kitchen window like some lingering fragrance? Or was it a depressed ghost that tried to possess my daughter and me?

I hear the distant drone of the Baker's Island foghorn some nights from my bedroom. It is like the lonesome wail of a banshee, and it makes me think about

101

the mysteries of the Wells Cottage and of the *"Party House,"* some few yards away on the bluff. As I listen I wonder, is a great black beast gathering its flock of wispy spirits to dance on the arched piazza, as disturbed seagulls and blackbirds circle dizzyingly overhead? Are strange gruesome ghosts from the bowels of the sea floating through the damp fog to clink glasses, mumble incoherently, and play soft music behind closed shutters of the Chase Cottage? Or is it quiet on Baker's Island, but for the blare of the foghorn and the lapping of the waves?

Be you a believer in ghosts or not, Baker's contains great mystery and charm and is truly a haunting place—truly *"an island of the sirens,"* as poet James Russell Lowell dubbed her. I may never visit Baker's Island again, but I shall never forget my experience there. It deepened my belief in the thin veil that separates this world from the world of spirits. The thought of unseen energies tied to specific locations often frightens me, probably because I don't understand it. Like our own world, however, it seems to contain both good and evil. Brian-the-monk still disagrees with me on this, believing that all ghosts are evil, or at least should not be trusted. Maybe he is right. Maybe they are all demons of the devil, but I feel I am a better man for meeting them and feeling their presence— and I did enjoy their company even if it was only for brief moments.

Ghosts have a way of stimulating me, like a cold shower or a good kick in the butt to make me appreciate being alive. Ghosts make me more aware that life isn't just birth, death and what's in between, but it's what comes after as well. I believe that if I'm active and full of good spirits while I'm alive here on earth, it goes without saying that I'll probably be a good spirit in the next world as well, when it's MY TURN to do the haunting!

Baker's Island

Frightened by what he called "a demon," on the third floor of the Wells Cottage at Baker's Island, Brian-the-monk quickly snapped this photo before he fled the cottage. Is this the demon-ghost, or does the photo show us only an illusion?